TEACHING IN THE CITY

SOCIAL RESEARCH SERIES, published in association with the Department of Social Science, University College, Dublin

TEACHING
IN THE CITY

A study of the role of the primary teacher

SEAN G. KELLY

GILL AND MACMILLAN

First published 1970

Gill and Macmillan
2 Belvedere Place
Dublin 1
and in London
through association with
Macmillan and Co. Ltd.

Cover design by Des Fitzgerald

7171 0250 5

Printed and bound in the Republic of Ireland
by Cahill and Co. Limited, Parkgate Street, Dublin

CONTENTS

PREFACE   viii

ACKNOWLEDGEMENTS   ix

LIST OF TABLES   xi

I PURPOSE AND SCOPE OF THE STUDY   1

Scope of the Study   3
Outline of the Report   5

II REVIEW OF THE LITERATURE RELATED
   TO THE STUDY   6

Studies of the Teacher's Role and the Theoretical
    Definition of Role   6
Writings on the Satisfactions and Dissatisfactions
    of Teachers   13
Studies of the Social Origins of Teachers   17
Conceptual Framework of the Study   19

III SITUATIONAL FRAMEWORK OF
    THE STUDY   22

The Irish System of National (Primary) Education 22
The Formal Definition of the Roles of National
    School Personnel   26
National Schools and Lay National Teachers in
    Dublin City   28

IV RESEARCH PROCEDURES USED IN THE
      STUDY   33

      Choice of Method for Gathering Data   33
      Construction of Postal Questionnaire   34
      Population Studied   34
      Sample   35
      Response Waves and the Effect of Reminders   36
      Response   37
      Analysis of Replies   37

V SOCIAL ORIGINS OF TEACHERS   38

      Social Group Origin of Respondents   38
      Geographical Origin of Respondents   41
      Social Origins of Teachers and Pupils   43

VI THE ROLE OF THE TEACHER   45

      Role Definition   45
      Role-Set   56
      Summary of the Role of the Teacher   63

VII PARENT-TEACHER RELATIONS   65

      Form and Extent of Existing Parent-Teacher
        Relations   67
      Attitude of Teachers to Parents   71
      Attitude of Teachers to Changes in Parent-
        Teacher Relations   74
      Conclusions and Implications   83

VIII SATISFACTIONS AND DISSATISFACTIONS
OF TEACHERS 86

Level of Satisfaction of Teachers 86
Factors Preventing Teachers from Achieving their
Ideals 92
Sources of Satisfaction and Dissatisfaction with
Various Aspects of Teaching 93
Reasons for Satisfaction or Dissatisfaction with
Various Aspects of Teaching 96
Conclusion 106

IX CONCLUSION 109

Pupil-Centred Teachers 110
The Role-Set of the Teacher 111
Parent-Teacher Relations 114
Job Satisfaction 115
Social Origins 118
Final Comments 119

APPENDIX 1 — Additional Tables 120

APPENDIX 2 — Questionnaire on Teaching 154

APPENDIX 3 — Statistical Notes 165

APPENDIX 4 — Further Tables 167

BIBLIOGRAPHY 169

PREFACE

SEAN G. KELLY, B.A., B.SOC.SC., DIP.PSYCH., M.SOC.SC.

SEAN KELLY was born in Co. Mayo. He trained as a National Teacher in St Patrick's, Drumcondra, and taught for some years in Clontarf National School. He took the B.A. degree and later the B.Soc.Sc. degree, the Diploma in Psychology with First Class Honours, and then went on to take the M.Soc.Sc. degree with First Class Honours in Autumn 1967. He was appointed an Assistant in the Social Science Department of U.C.D., but interrupted his work there to go to Cornell University for a Ph.D. Course in Sociology. Just before leaving for Cornell, he married Miss Mary Mulligan, who herself had obtained the M.Soc.Sc. degree with First Class Honours. He was accidentally drowned while swimming in the campus lake at Cornell on 28 July 1968.

Sean Kelly had shown himself a brilliant student and research worker and an excellent lecturer. At Cornell his studies were regarded as outstanding. Few would dispute the claim that by his death at the early age of 30, Ireland has lost a man of exceptional ability and charm.

This book is an indication of his profound grasp of the discipline of sociology.

JAMES KAVANAGH,
Professor of Social Science,
University College, Dublin.

ACKNOWLEDGEMENTS

In the course of preparing a piece of research one becomes indebted to many people. The book itself is based on the author's thesis presented to the National University of Ireland in 1967 for the degree of Master of Social Science. For help at all stages of this work the author is indebted to Rev. Professor James Kavanagh and to Rev. Dr Conor K. Ward, both of the Department of Social Science, University College, Dublin. In addition, he benefited from discussions with Senator Sean Brosnahan, M.A., H.Dip.Ed., Dip.Pub.Adm., General Secretary, Irish National Teachers' Organization and the late Mr Sean Perdisatt, B.Comm., Principal Officer, Department of Education.

The author would like to acknowledge the help of Professor Neal Gross of Harvard University not only for reading the final report and making detailed comments and suggestions, but also for his continual encouragement. He also acknowledges the help of Professors Gordon F. Streib and Robin M. Williams Jr. of Cornell University who made many useful suggestions on the final draft. He owes thanks also to Mr Paid McGee, B.A., H.Dip.Ed., Dip.Psych., Director, Department of Special Education, St Patrick's College, Dublin; Mr Domhnall O hUallachain, B.A., H.Dip.Ed., Chief Inspector, Primary Branch, Department of Education; and Miss Teresa Whitney, B.Soc.Sc., M.A., of the Department of Social Science, University College, Dublin, all of whom read the final thesis report. The fact that the final book version differs so much from what they read is an indication of their helpfulness.

In the mechanics of carrying out a survey the co-operation of many people is necessary. The author was fortunate in having the goodwill of the Dublin City Branch of the Irish National Teachers' Organization. He is particularly indebted to its secretary Mr Kevin Hurley, N.T., B.A., H.Dip.Ed. In addition, many members of The Teachers' Study Group gave him their assistance, particularly C. R. O'Connell, Declan McDonagh, Tim McGillicuddy, Vincent Greaney, Pat McNamara, and J. J. Quinn. The author would also like to thank the Computer Section of the Physics Department of University College, Dublin, for their help in analysing the data and to thank Eileen Scanlan, Evangeline McGee, Breda Downes, Maureen O'Callaghan and Mrs Churey for their courtesy and efficiency in typing the many drafts.

The author acknowledges the help of the I.N.T.O. both for their help in carrying out the survey and for their financial aid towards the preparation of the material for publication.

Acknowledgement is given to *The Irish Journal of Education* for permission to use, in Chapter VII, some material which originally appeared in *The Attitude of Teachers to Parent-Teacher Relations* in that journal (Vol. 1. No. 2, Winter 1967). The help of Rev. Dr John Macnamara, C.M. of St Patrick's College, Dublin, in connection with that article is acknowledged.

The author owes special thanks to the primary teachers in Dublin who were so obliging in answering the survey's questionnaire. Without their co-operation this book would never have been written.

SEAN G. KELLY.

Ithaca,
  June 1968.

LIST OF TABLES

Table		Page
3.1	Primary schools, pupils and teachers in the Republic of Ireland on 1 February 1964	24
3.2	Teachers in all national schools in the Republic of Ireland on 30 June 1965	24
3.3	Number of national schools, teachers, and pupils in national schools in Dublin City on 30 June 1965	29
3.4	Number and percentage of men and women (a) in Dublin City Branch, I.N.T.O. and (b) among respondents	31
3.5	Age of respondents compared with that of all lay national teachers in Ireland	31
4.1	Response waves	36
5.1	The occupation by social category of fathers of respondents	39
5.2	Percentage of fathers of (a) respondents, (b) lay students entering training colleges (1963), (c) leaving certificate candidates (1963), (d) university entrants (1963) who took the leaving certificate (1963), in three occupational categories compared with the percentage of each category in the basic population (1961)	40
5.3	Location of home of respondents' parents and of lay entrants to training colleges compared with percentage distribution of total population (1961)	42
5.4	Type of area from which the majority of the pupils taught by respondents came	44
6.1	Obligation felt by respondents to ensure that pupils perform religious duties	47
6.2	Mean ($\bar{X}$) and variance (V) of expectations of men, women and total on each item of role definition instrument	49

Table		*Page*
6.3	Degree of influence respondents felt is exercised on their work by incumbents of counter positions as indicated by mean ($\bar{X}$) and variance (V) for each counter position	58
6.4	Summary of respondents' perception of what was chiefly expected of them by incumbents of counter positions	60
7.1	Meetings of parents and teachers by place of meeting	68
7.2	Extent of respondents' contact at school with parents, related to type of area from which pupils came	69
7.3	Existence of parent-teacher associations or groups, related to the type of area from which pupils came	70
7.4	Degree of satisfaction with attitude of parents to education	71
7.5	Degree of satisfaction with relations with parents	72
7.6	Degree of contact respondents would like with parents and degree of contact they felt parents would like with them	74
7.7	Rank score and rank position of each form of parent-teacher relations	78
7.8	Number and percentage of respondents who ranked the given forms of parent-teacher relations first	79
8.1	Level of satisfaction of respondents with their work as teachers	87
8.2	Level of satisfaction related to type of area from which pupils of respondents came	88
8.3	Respondents' opinions as to whether teaching had lived up to their expectations	90
8.4	Advice respondents would give to their sons and daughters if they wished to become national teachers	91

Table   *Page*

8.5   Percentage of respondents who said that each of the following factors prevented them from achieving their ideals   92

8.6   Satisfaction-dissatisfaction scores ($\bar{X}$) and variances (V) on each item of the satisfaction-dissatisfaction check list   95

APPENDIX 1

A.1   Obligation to ensure pupils perform religious duties   121

A.2   Obligation to organize games for pupils after school   121

A.3   Obligation to send reports on pupils' progress to parents   122

A.4   Obligation to give individual attention to backward children   122

A.5   Obligation to invite parents of difficult pupils to come and see him (teacher)   122

A.6   Obligation to train pupils to think   123

A.7   Obligation to arrange parent-teacher meetings   123

A.8   Obligation to give good example to pupils by his behaviour outside school   123

A.9   Obligation to live in the parish he teaches in   124

A.10   Obligation to give special attention to very bright pupils   124

A.11   Obligation to teach the prescribed programme   124

A.12   Obligation to develop the moral character of his pupils   12

A.13   Obligation to try to ensure that pupils grow up good Christians   125

A.14   Obligation to develop in pupils a love of Ireland   125

A.15   Obligation to give good example to pupils by his behaviour in school   126

xivTEACHING IN THE CITY

Table *Page*

A.16 Obligation to help pupils become good members of society 126

A.17 Obligation to extend his teaching beyond the prescribed programme 126

A.18 Colleagues' influence on respondents' work 127

A.19 Parents' influence on respondents' work 127

A.20 Principals' influence on respondents' work 127

A.21 Pupils' influence on respondents' work 128

A.22 Managers' influence on respondents' work 128

A.23 Inspectors' influence on respondents' work 128

A.24 Mean, variance, standard deviation and standard error for tables A.1 to A. 23 129

A.25 Degree of contact respondents would like with parents, related to type of area from which pupils were drawn 129

A.26 Degree of satisfaction with parents' attitude to education related to type of area from which pupils came 130

A.27 Degree of satisfaction with relations with parents related to type of area from which pupils came 130

A.28 Factors preventing teachers from achieving their ideals related to type of area from which pupils came 131

A.29 Degree of contact male respondents would like with parents related to degree of contact they thought parents wanted with them 132

A.30 Degree of contact female respondents would like with parents related to degree of contact they thought parents wanted with them 132

A.31 Degree of contact respondents thought parents would like with them, related to type of area from which pupils were drawn 132

A.32 Percentage of respondents ranking (1-6) formal parent-teacher associations related to type of area from which pupils came 133

A.33 Number and percentage of respondents who ranked 'formal parent-teacher associations' 1 to 6 134

Table   *Page*

A.34 Number and percentage of respondents who
      ranked 'period of ordinary school time to be
      allotted to meeting parents' 1 to 6   134

A.35 Number and percentage of respondents who
      ranked 'no special arrangements but that the
      teacher sees parents if they call to the school'
      1 to 6   135

A.36 Number and percentage of respondents who
      ranked 'teachers to be available in the school
      one evening a month to meet parents' 1 to 6   135

A.37 Number and percentage of respondents who
      ranked 'special meeting to be called once or
      twice a year at which teacher, manager and
      parents are present' 1 to 6   136

A.38 Number and percentage of respondents who
      ranked 'no opportunity be given to parents of
      meeting the teacher' 1 to 6   136

A.39 Age and sex of respondents related to level of
      satisfaction   137

A.40 Comparison of (i) all respondents and (ii) res-
      pondents from poor city centre areas at each
      level of satisfaction, classified according to age
      and sex   138

A.41 Level of satisfaction of respondents whose pupils
      came from poor city centre areas related to sex   139

A.42 Percentage distribution of respondents over and
      under 40 years by level of satisfaction   139

A.43 Percentage distribution of respondents whose
      pupils came from poor city centre areas, over
      and under 40 years by level of satisfaction   139

A.44 Extent to which teaching had lived up to expec-
      tations related to age and sex of respondents   140

A.45 Advice respondents would give to daughters about
      becoming national teachers related to area from
      which respondents' pupils came   140

xvi TEACHING IN THE CITY

Table   *Page*

A.46 Advice respondents would give daughters about becoming national teachers, related to age and sex of respondents   141

A.47 Advice respondents would give sons about becoming national teachers, related to area from which respondents' pupils came   141

A.48 Advice respondents would give sons about becoming national teachers, related to age and sex of respondents   142

A.49 Factors which prevent achievement of ideals—pupils   142

A.50 Factors which prevent achievement of ideals—parents   143

A.51 Factors which prevent achievement of ideals—teaching aids   143

A.52 Factors which prevent achievement of ideals—curriculum   144

A.53 Factors which prevent achievement of ideals—management and administration of school   144

A.54 Factors which prevent achievement of ideals—class   145

A.55 Other factors which prevent achievement of ideals   145

A.56 Breakdown of the number of respondents classified by age and sex who said there were no factors preventing them from achieving their ideals   146

A.57 Satisfaction with relations with parents   146

A.58 Satisfaction with holidays   146

A.59 Satisfaction with curriculum   147

A.60 Satisfaction with salary   147

A.61 Satisfaction with hours of work   147

A.62 Satisfaction with size of class   148

A.63 Satisfaction with relations with inspector   148

A.64 Satisfaction with respect and recognition from the public   148

A.65 Satisfaction with relations with colleagues   149

A.66 Satisfaction with opportunities for promotion   149

A.67 Satisfaction with provision of teaching aids   149

Table   *Page*

A.68 Satisfaction with working with children   150
A.69 Satisfaction with relations with principal   150
A.70 Satisfaction with attitude of parents to education 150
A.71 Satisfaction with attitude of pupils to education 151
A.72 Satisfaction with discipline in school   151
A.73 Satisfaction with training for teaching   151
A.74 Satisfaction with relations with manager   152
A.75 Mean, variance, standard deviation and standard
        error for tables A.57 to A.74   152
A.76 Location of home at birth of respondents related
        to occupational category of father   153

APPENDIX 4

B.1   Number of lay and religious Catholic school units
        in the area covered by Dublin City Branch,
        I.N.T.O.   167
B.2   Number of teachers classified by type of school in
        Catholic school units in the area covered by
        Dublin City Branch, I.N.T.O.   167
B.3   Percentage distribution of lay and religious
        primary teachers in Catholic school units in the
        area covered by Dublin City Branch, I.N.T.O.   168
B.4   Percentage distribution of lay teachers in lay and
        religious Catholic school units in the area
        covered by Dublin City Branch, I.N.T.O.   168

CHAPTER I

PURPOSE AND SCOPE
OF THE STUDY

T H I S is a study of teachers. It was undertaken to achieve an understanding of how teachers perceived their work, work-relationships and work-difficulties. It focuses on teaching as an occupation. In the course of the study the views of teachers on their work were obtained and analysed within a sociological framework. Accordingly, it is a study in the field of the sociology of occupations, a relatively new field of sociology which has been defined as 'the application of sociological principles to the realm of work and occupational life'.[1]

Teachers, as a group, occupy a key position in society. It is their function to aid the development of subsequent generations by communicating to them a value system and preparing them for their place in society. Asher Tropp in the preface to his book on elementary teachers suggests that it is necessary to make '. . . studies of particular groups or professions . . . whose place in the structure of the community . . . could be regarded as "critical" '.[2] Teachers have such a 'critical' place in Irish society and thus warrant in a special way the attention of sociologists.

While the study was chiefly designed as a contribution to sociology, it was also carried out with the intention of providing useful information on one aspect of Irish education, namely the work of national teachers. These are primary teachers in national schools.[3] Before beginning the study the author, as a teacher and a member of teachers' organizations, had wide experience of the formal and informal setting of national

[1]S. Nosow and W. H. Form (Eds.), *Man, Work and Society*, New York, 1961, p. 3.
[2]A. Tropp, *The School Teachers*, London, 1957, p. viii.
[3]For a discussion of national schools see pp. 22-32.

teaching.[4] In 1964, two years before the study was undertaken, he left national teaching. Thus, while his experience of national teaching was useful in planning the study, the author felt he was sufficiently removed from the immediate situation of teaching to carry out an objective investigation.

An increasing amount of empirical information on Irish education is becoming available. It covers principally standards of achievement,[5] social factors in education,[6] economic aspects of education,[7] and statistical data on teachers and pupils.[8] This book supplements the statistical data on teachers in Ireland by concentrating on the attitudes and opinions of teachers in relation to their work. It also sets out to compare the results of this investigation with those of some similar studies of teachers in England and the United States, though no attempt is made to include all such American or British studies in this review.

This study, then, is a contribution to the sociology of occupations. It goes beyond this, however, in that the occupation studied is a key one in society and so the study may provide some insight into the functioning of society as a whole. In addition, by giving some attention to the position of the teacher within the social structure of the school, some light is thrown on the functioning of social organizations. The study may also contribute to an understanding of education in Ireland by providing information on some of the teachers in its primary schools.

[4]Between 1959 and 1964 the author taught as a national teacher in Dublin city. He was a founder member of the Teachers' Study Group (1961), and a member of the committee of the Dublin City Branch, Irish National Teachers' Organization (1962-64).

[5]See: S. Kelly and P. McGee, 'Survey of Reading Comprehension—a study in Dublin city national schools,' *New Research in Education*, Vol. 1, May 1967, pp. 131-134. See also: J. Macnamara, *Bilingualism and Primary Education—a study of Irish experience*, Edinburgh, 1966.

[6]See: K. Cullen, *School and Family*, Dublin, 1969; M. J. Mulligan *Youth in a Country Town*, unpublished M.Soc.Sc. Thesis, University College, Dublin, 1967; M. Nevin, *A Study of the Social Background of Students in University College, Dublin,* paper read before the Statistical and Social Inquiry Society of Ireland, Dublin, 27 January 1967; L. Ryan, 'Social Dynamite—a study of early school leavers', *Christus Rex*, Vol. XXI, No. 1, Spring 1967, pp. 7-44; C. K. Ward, *Manpower in a Developing Community*, Abridged Report, Dublin, 1967.

[7]See: *Investment in Education*, Report, Dublin, 1965; also *Investment in Education, Annexes and Appendices*, Dublin, 1966.

[8]See: An Roinn Oideachais, *Turascail, Tablai Staitistic, 1964-65*, Dublin, 1966; P. Duffy, *The Lay Teacher*, Dublin, 1967.

Scope of the Study

In January 1966 the author began to explore the possibility of a study of national teachers. Having read much of the related literature and having discussed with some teachers the possible success of various research procedures, he formulated a number of questions which explored what teachers felt was the essence of their work and the problems which made the achievement of their ideals difficult. It appeared from the answers to these questions and from the fact that many of the teachers said they would welcome such a study that a survey of national teachers would be valuable.

It was decided to concentrate on three major areas of study: the teacher's role, social origins and work satisfactions. Taken together these form a coherent picture of some of the sociological aspects of teachers' work.

One of the major dimensions of a study of the members of any profession or work group is the members' perception of the obligations of their job and the activities which they feel others in related positions expect from them. Role is the sociological concept which unifies such ideas and in this study the role of the teacher is explored in terms of how he feels he is obliged and expected to behave. The concept role-set is used to refer to the relationships which teachers have with others occupying related positions, such as the school manager, principal or parents. This study pays particular attention to parents and also considers to some extent the whole authority system within which the teacher works.

The social origins of teachers are also studied. Information on social origins helps to locate teachers as a group in the social structure by investigating their environmental and cultural backgrounds.

Finally, the satisfactions and dissatisfactions of teachers with their work are investigated. An attempt is made to identify the degree of their satisfaction with teaching and to pinpoint the sources of their satisfactions or dissatisfactions.

All studies of this kind have limitations. This study is confined to a sample of lay national teachers in Dublin city schools on 1 October 1966. While the findings may have relevance for national teachers in other parts of Ireland, or for religious national teachers in Dublin city,[9] these are outside the population studied and consequently results may not be generalized to them. For convenience, however, the word 'teachers' is often used in the text to mean the population of this study, i.e. lay national teachers in Dublin city. Where any other category of teacher is meant, this is specifically stated.

The study is also circumscribed conceptually and methodologically. In a survey of this kind it is not possible to investigate all aspects of teaching and the researcher must confine himself to what appear to be the most relevant aspects of his subject. In addition, he may not be able to give full consideration to the history of the topic under investigation. This is not to say that historical considerations are unimportant, and it is hoped that, in this instance, other publications will fill the lacuna.[10] In the analysis of replies of respondents it was not possible to consider all the variables which might have influenced the variation in response. The replies of men and women were always analysed separately and then compared. It would have been interesting to have related all replies to such queries as size of school and age of respondents, but this could only be done occasionally.

It is hoped that the findings will be of interest to many people in addition to professional social scientists. It is expected that teachers will find some of their problems articulated, if not solved, in this book. Student teachers should find it a useful introduction to what life is like in their chosen profession. Many parents may find the book useful in helping them to understand how a school works. It is hoped that the book will be of special interest to school managers, Department of Education officials and leaders of the Irish National Teachers' Organization, all of whom are directly concerned with the more efficient working of the educational system.

[9]For the purposes of this study national teachers who are religious brothers or sisters are referred to as religious teachers, as opposed to lay teachers.

[10]A good brief history of teachers in Ireland is contained in Duffy, *op. cit.* In addition, it is understood that a history of the Irish National Teachers' Organization is being prepared.

Outline of the Report

Chapters II, III and IV present respectively the conceptual, situational and methodological frameworks within which this study was carried out. Chapter II contains the sociological definitions of the concepts used in the study and a review of the literature from Britain and America in which these concepts were used in previous investigations of teachers and their work. This review should be of special interest to Irish teachers, who may be pleased to find that their problems are not unique. Chapter III presents a description of the Irish system of national (primary) education, mainly for the benefit of readers outside Ireland who may have difficulty in understanding the system within which the subjects of this study work. Chapter IV is devoted exclusively to an account of the research methods used in the study. A description of the research methods might, perhaps, have been confined to an appendix, but it was felt that since the actual research methods used are of central importance in reports of social surveys their inclusion in the text of the report was warranted.

Results of the survey are given in Chapters V to VIII. The social origins of teachers are dealt with in Chapter V; role is discussed in Chapter VI; a more detailed examination of one relationship in the role-set, relations with parents, is discussed in Chapter VII; while teachers' satisfactions and dissatisfactions are studied in Chapter VIII.

In Chapter IX, an attempt is made to interpret the findings; and some implications of the study are also discussed in relation to suggestions for further research. The appendices include additional tables not presented in the text, a copy of the questionnaire used and statistical notes.

CHAPTER II

REVIEW OF THE LITERATURE
RELATED TO THE STUDY

A NECESSARY part of any scientific study is a review of the literature related to the theme of the research. In this way new findings can be placed within the context of existing knowledge and their significance better assessed. Much has been written on the theme of this research, and this chapter reviews the literature relating to: (1) the development of the concept of role and its use in the analysis of the position of the teacher; (2) the satisfactions and dissatisfactions of teachers; and (3) the social origins of teachers. Drawing on this literature the conceptual framework of this study is then described.

Accordingly, this chapter is divided into four sections:
I Studies of the teacher's role and the theoretical definition of role;
II Writings on the satisfactions and dissatisfactions of teachers;
III Studies of the social origins of teachers;
IV Conceptual framework of the study.

Studies of the Teacher's Role and the Theoretical Definition of Role
This section reviews some non-empirical writings on the teacher's job and also sets out to examine the sociological concept of role in order to show how it can make explicit some of the problems which teachers encounter in their work.

1. *Non-Empirical Writings on Teachers.* The central concern of the more important non-empirical writings on the teacher's role has been the variability of his role obligations and the degree of personal commitment which he needs for the effective performance of his work.

6

Perhaps the most extensive treatment of the role of the teacher, at this level of analysis, is contained in *The Teacher's Role in American Society*.[1] In Chapter VI of this book Jean D. Grambs says that the teacher has two main categories of roles: teacher as director of learning, and teacher as mediator of culture.[2] As director of learning, Grambs says two kinds of things are expected of him in the process of teaching. While he must judge achievement, keep discipline and establish a moral atmosphere, he is expected at the same time to be confidant and guide, and giver of advice and affection. His role of mediator of culture, Grambs says, arises from the social function of education. In concluding this discussion Grambs describes the roles of the teacher as 'many and contradictory'.[3]

On the same notion of variability in the tasks which a teacher is expected to perform, Oeser observes:

> A mechanic has only one role in relation to his machines: to fit new parts and repair old ones. A teacher has many roles in relation to his pupils. Their range and the complexity of their interrelations make the teacher's task intrinsically one of the most interesting in the world and one of the most difficult, satisfying, and sometimes, nevertheless, frustrating.[4]

He goes on to list the main roles of the teacher, in dealing with pupils, as follows: (a) instructor, clarifier and expert; (b) judge of achievements and assessor; (c) ethical preceptor and moralist; (d) legislator; (e) judge; (f) policeman; and (g) friend and counsellor.

A rather similar comment is made in the *Plowden Report* on the role of the teacher within the English educational system:

> So broad and ill-defined a role is almost bound to be at one and the same time satisfying and yet over-demanding.

[1] L. J. Stiles (Ed.), *The Teacher's Role in American Society*, New York, 1957.
[2] J. D. Grambs, *The Roles of the Teacher*, in Stiles (Ed.), *ibid*, pp. 73-93.
ibid., p. 85.
[4] O. A. Oeser, *Teacher, Pupil and Task*, London, 1955, p. 5.

The teacher's work can never be seen to be completed. Its outcome is usually undramatic, and success can never be finally or tidily assessed.[5]

Bryan Wilson also describes this multiplicity of roles which the teacher performs.[6] He says that teaching, which involves motivating, inspiring, encouraging and transmitting values, is unspecific. The role obligation is diffuse and difficult to delimit, and the activities of the role are highly diverse. In other professional roles such as those of the doctor, dentist or lawyer a definable expertise is involved but in teaching there are distinct limits to the extent of specialization possible.

Other writers on the role of the teacher have emphasized the degree to which the teacher is judged on his personal attributes rather than on his more specific qualifications as a teacher. Wilbur Brookover in his book, *A Sociology of Education*, suggests that 'perhaps the first requisite of the teacher in America is that he or she must "set a good example"'.[7] A similar statement was made of the teacher in England in the *Plowden Report*:

It has long been characteristic of the English educational system that the teacher has been expected to carry the burden of teaching by example as well as by precept. He is expected to be a good man and to influence children more by what he is than by what he knows or by his methods.[8]

These non-empirical writings on teachers have tended to describe the kind of job or functions which the teacher is expected to perform. The insights provided by these studies have a useful indicative function in that they point to areas which might be fruitfully investigated in an empirical study.

[5]Central Advisory Council for Education (England), *Children and Their Primary Schools* (Plowden Report), Vol. 1, London, 1967, p. 312.

[6]B. Wilson, 'The Teacher's Role—a sociological analysis', in *British Journal of Sociology*, Vol. XIII, No. 1, March 1962, pp. 15-32.

[7]W. Brookover, *A Sociology of Education*, New York, 1955, p. 345.

[8]Plowden Report, *op. cit.*, p. 311.

2. *The Sociological Concept of Role and its Application to Studies of Teachers.* One of the concepts which has been used in empirical investigations of teachers and their work is that of role.[9] In many ways, the concept of role emerged, through a process of gradual refinement, from a stage where it was loosely used to highlight insights into the functioning of society to the point where it was defined operationally and actually used in scientific investigation.[10]

Ralph Linton, an anthropologist, was one of the first to use role as a key concept in social science.[11] He defined role as: '... the sum total of culture patterns associated with a particular status',[12] or position. It consists of '... attitudes, values and behaviour ascribed by society to any and all persons occupying this status.'[13] Thus, for Linton, a role referred to socially and culturally prescribed norms for behaviour in a particular position, or in other words what ought to be done by all incumbents of a given status. For Linton, the role of the teacher would consist of the pattern of behaviour prescribed by society for teachers. Linton did not perceive the possibility of the members of society making conflicting demands on the occupants of a position. As an anthropologist his frame of reference was a small, traditional, closed society where one set of norms defining appropriate behaviour in a particular position may be more likely to exist than in modern, complex societies.

The possibility of conflicting demands being made on the incumbents of a position was recognized by Robert Merton. In his book, *Social Theory and Social Structure*, he queries Linton's statement that each status has its distinctive role. He points out that '... a particular social status involves, not a single asso-

---

[9]The term 'role' is used here rather than 'role theory'. This writer would be inclined to reserve 'role theory' for the psychological orientation to personality development, which sees the development of personality largely as the process of socialization through the acceptance of roles. Relevant contributions to this study are, of course, accepted whether under the heading 'role' or 'role theory'.

[10]For a more detailed presentation see: S. Kelly, *Role, Social Origins and Satisfactions of Lay National Teachers in Dublin City—A Study in the Sociology of Occupations*, M.Soc.Sc. Thesis, University College, Dublin, 1967.

[11]R. Linton, *The Study of Man*, New York, 1936.

[12]R. Linton, *The Cultural Background of Personality*, New York, 1945, p. 77.

[13]*Ibid.*, p. 77.

ciated role, but an array of associated roles'[14] and continues: 'This fact of a structure can be registered by a distinctive term, role-set . . .'[15] He defines role-set as '. . . that complement of role relationships which persons have by virtue of occupying a particular social status'.[16] One of the examples he gives is the status (position) of public school teacher which he says has its

> . . . distinctive role-set, relating the teacher to his pupils, to colleagues, the school principal and superintendent, the Board of Education and on frequent occasions to local patriotic organizations, to professional organizations of teachers, Parent-Teacher associations and the like.[17]

Thus for Merton each role is related to a structured set of other roles. Appropriate behaviour in a given role is not conditioned by a single cultural norm but rather by the normative expectations of the incumbents in the other positions related to this role, i.e., the role-set. Those in the role-set may not hold similar normative expectations of what is appropriate behaviour in a given position, and therefore the incumbent of this position may be open to differing expectations of how he ought to behave.

Further refinements in the definition of the concept of role were made by Neal Gross and his associates, who took up Linton's concept of role and attempted to redefine it and its related concepts in operational terms.[18] They worked out a series of role concepts, and an explication of four of them will be presented below. These are: (i) Position, (ii) Expectations, (iii) Role, and (iv) Role behaviour.

(i) *Position*. Gross uses the term position much as others, such as Linton, used the term status. By position he means '. . . the location of an actor or class of actors in a system of social

[14]R. K. Merton, *Social Theory and Social Structure*, New York, 1957, p. 369.
[15]*Ibid.*, p. 369.
[16]*Ibid.*, p. 369.
[17]*Ibid.*, p. 369.
[18]N. Gross, W. S. Mason and A. W. McEachern, *Explorations in Role Analysis—studies of the school superintendency role*, New York, 1958, see especially Chap. 4. 'A Language for Role Analysis', pp. 48-69.

relationships.'[19] Gross suggests that points in a system of social relationships acquire 'labels'. 'Teacher' and 'husband' are examples of such labels. Position, then, indicates the label of a point within a relationship system, rather than its behaviour pattern. In carrying out empirical research the position being studied must therefore be carefully specified. Gross discusses two aspects of position specification: relational and situational. The relational specification of positions implies relations to other positions, and Gross shows that '. . . it is necessary for an investigator in focusing on one position (focal position), to specify the other positions (counter positions) with which his analysis will be concerned.'[20] In a study of teacher as a focal position, such counter positions as parent, pupil or principal could be examined. The situational specification of a position concerns the geographical and institutional system in which the position is studied.

(ii) *Expectations*. Gross defines expectation as '. . . an evaluative standard applied to an incumbent of a position.'[21] It is thus used in a normative sense to express a standard or judgment of what should be. Expectations have two dimensions: (a) Direction—they are for or against something; (b) Intensity—they can vary on a scale from being mandatory to being completely permissive.

(iii) *Role*. 'A role is a set of expectations, or in terms of our definition of expectations, it is a set of evaluative standards applied to an incumbent of a particular position.'[22] This definition can be used at any level of relational and situational specificity which can be applied to a given position.[23] Also, as Gross shows, this definition permits the investigation of consensus on role as it leaves open the question of role definers, so that any individual, category, or group can be chosen as role definers for the purposes of a particular piece of research. Differences in the expectations held by various definers can then be investigated.

[19]*Ibid.*, p. 48.
[20]*Ibid.*, p. 50.
[21]*Ibid.*, p. 58.
[22]*Ibid.*, p. 60.
[23]*Ibid.*, p. 60.

(iv) *Role Behaviour*. Gross defines role behaviour as the actual performance of an incumbent of a position which can be related to what is expected of him in that position.

Thus Gross makes an important contribution to resolving the problems of role analysis by working out a series of operational concepts. Gross used these concepts and validated their utility in his study and analysis of the school superintendent's role.[24] These concepts have also been used by William Kuvlesky and Roy Buck[25] and by Louis Cohen[26] to analyse the role of the teacher.

Empirical studies investigating the problems teachers encounter in the United States and in Britain have used both Merton's concept of role-set and Gross's series of role concepts. Usually these studies have concluded either that there is little consensus among the different positions in the role-set concerning the teacher's role, or that, while there tends to be consensus on some aspects of the teacher's role, there is much less consensus on other aspects.[27] Lack of consensus means that different positions in the teacher's role-set hold differing expectations of how the teacher ought to behave. The teacher, these studies suggest, is caught in the centre of a web of conflicting demands and expectations which he finds difficult to resolve and which cause him anxiety and dissatisfaction.

3. *Conclusion*. Both the non-empirical and empirical studies presented above have indicated (1) that the teacher's role is not specific and that he has to play many diverse roles, and (2) that

[24]N. Gross et al., *Explorations in Role Analysis, op. cit.*

[25]William P. Kuvlesky and Roy C. Buck, *The Teacher-Student Relationship*, Pennsylvania State University, 1960.

[26]L. Cohen, *An Exploratory Study of the Teacher's Role as Perceived by Headteachers, Tutors, and Students in a Training College*, M.Ed. Thesis, University of Liverpool, 1965.

[27]See B. J. Biddle, S. Eveloff, E. Franklin Jr., H. A. Rosencranz, P. Twyman and D. Warshay, *Studies in the Role of the Public School Teacher*, Series II and III Empirical Reports, Columbia, University of Missouri, 1961; also C. Washbourne, *Involvement as a Basis for Stress Analysis—a study of high school teachers*, East Lansing, Michigan State College, doctoral dissertation, 1953, cited in Brookover, *op. cit.*, pp. 280–285; also C. Wayne Gordon, 'The Role of the Teacher in the Social Structure of the High School', in R. Bell (Ed.), *The Sociology of Education*, Illinois, 1962, pp. 327–336. See also William P. Kuvlesky and Roy C. Buck, *op. cit.*; and L. Cohen, *op. cit.*

the teacher is at the centre of conflicting expectations from those in his role-set. In order to study these aspects of the teacher's role in Dublin, Gross's definition of position, expectation and role, and Merton's definition of role-set were adopted. The fourth section of this chapter describes how each of these concepts was integrated into the conceptual framework of the study.

Writings on the Satisfactions and Dissatisfactions of Teachers

The term job satisfaction has been defined as the '. . . affective orientations on the part of individuals towards work roles which they are presently occupying.'[28] It is 'typically measured by means of interviews or questionnaires in which workers are asked to state the degree to which they like or dislike various aspects of their work'.[29] Workers may be asked in a general way whether they like or dislike their work, or alternatively they may be given a set of variables concerning their work and asked to specify whether or not they are satisfied with each of these. In this second method of analysis job satisfaction is '. . . treated as a set of dimensions rather than a single dimension . . .'[30] Some of the major dimensions of job satisfaction which have been investigated are supervision, the work group, job content, wages, promotional opportunities, and hours of work.[31]

These dimensions have been studied in terms of the job satisfaction of teachers both in Britain and in the United States. It would appear from these investigations that job content is a key aspect of teachers' satisfaction or dissatisfaction with their work. Almost invariably it has been concluded that teachers find that relations with pupils, perhaps the defining feature of a teacher's job, are a chief source of satisfaction.[32] The lack of

[28]H. Vroom, *Work and Motivation*, New York, 1964, p. 99.
[29]*Ibid.*, p. 100.
[30]*Ibid.*, p. 101.
[31]*Ibid.*, p. 105.
[32]See R. G. Kuhlen, *Career Development in the Public School Teaching Profession with Special Reference to Changing Motivations, Pressures, Satisfactions and Dissatisfactions*, New York, Syracuse University Institute of Research, 1959; also T. Bienenstok and W. C. Sayres, *Problems in Job Satisfaction among Junior High School Teachers*, New York 1963; W. S. Mason, *The Beginning Teacher*, Washington, 1961.

facilities which might aid teaching has been found to be the chief source of dissatisfaction, and teachers most frequently complain of large classes, heavy teaching loads, and inadequate teaching materials.[33]

The teacher is related to three categories of persons, besides pupils, while in his work role. These are colleagues, supervisors and parents. Studies of teachers in the United States have concluded that teachers tend to be satisfied with these relationships.[34] To quote Ward Mason:

> There is a nearly unanimous feeling that all these relationships (with fellow teachers, superiors, students and parents) are satisfactory, and in each case a majority of teachers say 'very satisfactory'.[35]

It appears, however, that such satisfactory relationships do not always exist in Britain. W. G. A. Rudd and S. Wiseman who examined job satisfaction among teachers in England and Wales found that 'poor human relations' were the second greatest source of dissatisfaction for the teachers they studied.[36]

Studies of the job satisfaction of teachers have found that they tend to be dissatisfied with their remuneration,[37] although they are not usually as dissatisfied with it as they are with inadequate teaching facilities.[38] It has been suggested that teachers are dissatisfied with their pay because it does not enable them to live at the level at which they feel they are expected to live. To quote J. W. Getzels and E. G. Guba:

[33]See R. G. Kuhlen. *op. cit.*, also T. Bienenstok and W. C. Sayres, *op. cit.*, and W. G. A. Rudd and S. Wiseman, 'Sources of Dissatisfaction among a Group of Teachers,' *The British Journal of Educational Psychology*, Vol. XXXII, November 1962, pp. 275-291.

[34]See R. G. Kuhlen, *op. cit.*, also T. Bienenstok and W. C. Sayres, *op. cit.*, and W. S. Mason, *op. cit.*

[35]W. Mason, *op. cit.*, p. 79.

[36]W. G. A. Rudd and S. Wiseman, *op. cit.*

[37]R. G. Kuhlen, *op. cit.*; also T. Bienenstok and W. C. Sayres, *op. cit.*, W. Mason, *op. cit.*, and W. G. A. Rudd and S. Wiseman, *op. cit.*

[38]See R. G. Kuhlen, *op. cit.*; and T. Bienenstok and W. C. Sayres, *op. cit.*

In most communities teachers are assumed to be members of at least a quasi-professional group for whom middle-class standards of living are expected. However, in comparison with persons for whom similar standards are required, the teacher receives remuneration inadequate for conforming to these expectations.[39]

In general, it has been found that male teachers tend to be more dissatisfied than female teachers with teaching at the general level and also with salary and promotion opportunities.[40] Male teachers also tend to be more dissatisfied with the status of the teaching profession. Bienenstok and Sayres, having studied the job satisfaction of junior high school teachers, suggest that this may arise from the fact that

... men tend to be more demanding than women in what they expect from a job, since occupational roles are more important to them in defining 'what a man is' in the society, and since they are the primary winners and sources of family status.[41]

Getzels and Guba point out that as

... teaching is often thought of as a woman's profession is is not surprising to find that men should be more liable to conflicts in the teaching situation than women.[42]

In general it would appear from the above studies of teachers that greater dissatisfaction is caused by the lack of facilities which might aid teaching than by low salaries, although low salaries are also a source of anxiety and complaint, especially

---

[39] J. W. Getzels and E. G. Guba, 'The Structure of Roles and Role Conflict in the Teaching Situation', *The Journal of Educational Sociology*, Vol. 29, Sept. 1955, p. 31. See also International Labour Office, *Meeting the Experts on Teachers' Problems*, Geneva, 1958.
[40] See T. Bienenstok and W. C. Sayres, *op. cit.*, W. G. A. Rudd and S. Wiseman, *op. cit.*, and R. G. Kuhlen, *op. cit.*
[41] T. Bienenstok and W. C. Sayres, *op. cit.*, p. 37.
[42] J. W. Getzels and E. G. Guba, *op. cit.*, p. 39.

B

among men. Generally, relations with pupils are a major source of satisfaction, as are relations with colleagues and supervisors. Men appear to be more dissatisfied than women, especially as regards salary and opportunities for promotion.

Similar empirical studies on the satisfactions and dissatisfactions of teachers in Ireland have not been undertaken. However, some articles which refer to Irish national (primary) teachers have indicated possible areas of dissatisfaction.[43] Diarmuid O'Briain, writing in 1962, stated:

> ... it is probably true to say that never has there been such widespread and deep dissatisfaction among national teachers as there has been in the past five years. This dissatisfaction has two main causes: (1) the unhealthy state of primary education and (2) the losing battle of salaries against the cost of living.[44]

He went on to call for a realistic attack on the

> ... problems which bedevil the work of the schools, and because of which the results achieved are out of all proportion to the labour involved for teachers and pupils.
>
> In the present context all that can be done with those problems is to list them in approximate order of urgency. They are (1) Size of classes (2) The educationally retarded child (including retardation whether for reasons of mental or physical abnormality) despite the progress which has been made in this field (3) The question of research and experimentation in education (4) The training of teachers and Training College-University relationships (5) The Primary Certificate (6) Teaching aids and Textbooks (7) Suitability of school-buildings and furnishings; up-keep of same (8) School-Home liaison (9) Lack of

[43]J. Brosnahan, 'The Sins of our Primary Education', *An Muinteoir Naisiunta*, Iml. 1, Uimh. 2, Feabhra 1956, pp. 18-26, agus Iml. 1, Uimh. 2., Marta 1956, pp. 10-12; and D. O'Briain, 'Programme for Expansion', *An Muinteoir Naisiunta*, Iml. 7, Uimh. 9, Deire Fomhair 1962, pp. 8-11.
[44]D. O'Briain, *op. cit.*, p. 8.

freedom of movement between different types of schools for teachers suitably qualified, lack of liaison between upper reaches of primary school and lower reaches of secondary and vocational.[45]

Thus it can be seen that many of the problems cited by O'Briain are similar to those found to cause teacher dissatisfaction in Britain and the United States and the present study will investigate them systematically.

Studies of the Social Origins of Teachers

The social origins of teachers have been studied for two reasons. The first is to investigate whether teachers and pupils come from similar social backgrounds. This is thought to be of importance because of suggestions that the extent to which teachers can communicate with their pupils depends on the social background of pupils and teachers. The second is to investigate the degree to which teachers are upwardly mobile.

Sociologists have usually defined and examined the social origins of teachers in terms of the socio-economic class of teachers' fathers. It has been suggested that if teachers differ in class origins from the social class of their pupils this might cause difficulty of communication because of the lack of a common value system. On this theme, Wattenberg and Havinghurst write:

> There are within various socio-economic groups different patterns of upbringing.
>
> These find expression in somewhat contrasting personal value systems. Such facts give special interest to any study of the social origins of teachers, for at least two pressing questions need to be answered: What modes of behaviour and value systems are exemplified by teachers? How well equipped is the present teaching staff to understand, to sympathize, with children of different origins?[46]

[45]*Ibid.*, p. 9.
[46]W. Wattenberg and R. J. Havinghurst, 'The American Teacher—Then and Now', in L. J. Stiles (Ed.), *op. cit.*, p. 6.

Robert Bell suggests that

> The conflict of social class values enters into many areas of education. Such value assumptions of the middle-class teacher as thrift, respect for property, cleanliness, and sexual morality may not be shared by the lower-class student.[47]

The lower-class student may not hold education in such high esteem as his teacher. Bell remarks that there should be 'an awareness of the inherent value conflict in which the lower-class student is often caught.'[48] The student may be '. . . tugged in opposite directions, one way by the teacher and the school and in the opposite direction by the family and the peer group.'[49]

In the United States and in England and Wales studies of the social origins of teachers have been undertaken, from which it would appear that teachers in these countries come from a wide range of social backgrounds and that about 30 to 40 per cent come from working-class homes and are thus upwardly mobile.[50] The percentage of upwardly mobile teachers is greater if those from lower middle-class backgrounds (such as clerks and salesmen) are included. There appears to be a tendency for male teachers to come from a lower class background than female teachers.

Data on the social origins of teachers in Ireland are not available, though some information can be obtained from a study which investigated the social origins of lay students admitted to training colleges for primary teachers in 1963.[51] In this study it was found that 15 per cent of these students came from working-

[47]R. Bell, op. cit., p. 254.
[48]Ibid., p. 257.
[49]Ibid., p. 257.
[50]See W. W. Wattenberg et al., 'Social Origins of Teachers—a Northern Industrial City', in L. J. Stiles (Ed.), op. cit., pp. 13-22; also C. McGuire and G. White, 'Social Origins of Teachers in Texas', in L. J. Stiles (Ed.), Ibid., pp. 23-41, W. W. Wattenberg et al., 'Social Origins of Teachers and American Education', in L. J. Stiles (Ed.), ibid.; W. Mason, op. cit.; and J. Floud and W. Scott, 'Recruitment to Teaching in England and Wales,' in A. H. Halsey, J. Floud and C. A. Anderson (Eds.), Education, Economy, and Society, New York, 1961, pp. 527-544.
[51]Investment in Education, p. 6.

class homes, although the working-class population constitutes 40 per cent of the general population. Thirty per cent came from white-collar groups which constitute 20 per cent of the basic population. It would thus appear that primary teachers in Ireland are selected from particular social groups. This point will be investigated further in the course of this study.

Conceptual Framework of the Study

This section describes the conceptual framework of the study. The sociological literature related to the three main areas of this study, (1) role; (2) satisfactions and dissatisfactions of teachers; and (3) social origins of teachers has been reviewed above. The precise aspects of this literature and the definitions taken from it which are used in this study are presented below.

1. *Role.* The chief theoretical focus of this study is the concept of role. Two aspects of this concept are examined: role definition and role-set.

(a) *Role definition.* Gross's definition of role as '. . . a set of expectations applied to an incumbent of a particular position'[52] was adopted. Expectation, for Gross, is '. . . an evaluative standard applied to an incumbent of a position'.[53] The position chosen for investigation here was that of the lay national teacher in Dublin city. The use of the above definition of the concept role permits the researcher to choose any set of role definers he wishes. They may be the actual incumbents of the position under investigation, incumbents of related positions or simply 'unrelated others' in society. In this study lay national teachers, themselves the incumbents of the position under investigation, were chosen as role definers. Thus, the role definition aspect of the study is concerned with how national teachers define their role, i.e. what teachers think they ought to do as teachers.

(b) *Role-set.* Merton defined role-set as '. . . that complement of role relationships which persons have by virtue of occupying a particular social status (position)'.[54] The position of national

[52]N. Gross, W. Mason and A. McEachern, *op. cit.*, p. 67.
[53]*Ibid.*, p. 58.
[54]Merton, *op. cit.*, p. 369.

teacher in Dublin is related to many other positions of which the more important are: parent, pupil, inspector, colleague, principal and manager. There are other related positions, such as school attendance officer, but it was possible to examine only the more important ones.

Thus the role-set dimension of the study examines the relationship of the teacher with parents, pupils, inspectors, colleagues, principals and managers. In furthering this analysis Gross's position-centric model is useful.[55] He uses the term 'focal position' to specify the particular position under investigation, and the term 'counter position' to signify other related positions. For purposes of this study the focal position is that of lay national teacher in Dublin city, while the counter positions are those of manager, inspector, principal, pupil, parent and colleague. This can be diagrammatically represented as follows:

(Counter positions)

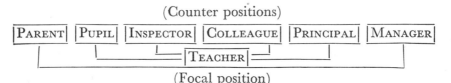

(Focal position)

One approach to a study of the relationship between the teacher and the above counter positions would be to interview a sample of incumbents of each of the counter positions and question them on their relationship with the teacher. Another approach is to question incumbents of the focal position about their relationship with incumbents of each of the counter positions. This latter is the approach adopted in this study.

For practical reasons it was not possible to investigate completely the relationships between the teacher and each of the six chosen counter positions. Accordingly, it was decided to take one counter position and investigate it more intensively. For this purpose the counter position of parent was chosen.

To summarize, the role dimension of this study has two aspects: (a) role definition, i.e., teachers' definition of their role or, to put it another way, how teachers think they ought to behave

[55]N. Gross, W. Mason, and A. McEachern, *op. cit.*, p. 52.

as teachers, (b) role-set, i.e., the relationship between teachers and incumbents of related counter positions; in this case the relationships between teachers and parents, pupils, inspector, colleagues, principal and manager.

2. *Satisfactions and Dissatisfactions of Teachers*. Satisfaction with teaching was studied from several viewpoints, and the following approaches were taken:[56] (a) a global measure of satisfaction with teaching was obtained, (b) a multidimensional checklist of aspects of teaching was presented to respondents and they were asked to rate their satisfaction or dissatisfaction with each item on the checklist, (c) respondents were asked if there were any aspects of teaching which prevented them from achieving their ideals as teachers, (d) they were asked if teaching had lived up to the expectations they had of it before taking it up as a career, and (e) they were asked whether they would advise their sons or daughters to become teachers.

By using these different approaches it was felt that the sources of teachers' satisfaction and dissatisfaction could be located in addition to obtaining an overall measure of their satisfaction and dissatisfaction.

3. *Social Origins of Teachers*. Two approaches to the study of social origins were adopted. Firstly, the social class of each respondent's father was examined. Secondly, the location of the respondent's home was considered with reference to the county in which he was born. Geographical origin was thus included for investigation since it was felt that under the heading of social origins more than social class should be considered. If there are regional variations in culture, then the geographical origins of teachers could be as important a dimension of their social origin as their class. Failure in communication between people of different classes would be accentuated if these people also came from different sub-cultures. Accordingly a two-dimensional concept of social origins was developed; class origin and geographical origin. Together, it was felt, these two indices would give a more complete picture of the social origins of teachers in Dublin city.

[56]The exact questions asked are given in the copy of the questionnaire reproduced in Appendix 2.

CHAPTER III

SITUATIONAL FRAMEWORK OF THE STUDY

THIS chapter describes the Irish system of primary education, with particular emphasis on Dublin city, which was the situational framework within which the study was carried out. The chapter is divided into three sections. The first presents information on the formal organization of the Irish system of national (primary) education and gives statistics on the numbers and types of national schools and the number and training of the teachers who staff them. The second section deals with the roles of the principal, manager, inspector and teacher in Irish national schools as formally defined by the Department of Education. The third section discusses the structure and staffing of national schools in Dublin city using both data gathered in this study and data from other sources.

The Irish System of National (Primary) Education[1]

Education is compulsory in Ireland for all children between the ages of 6 and 14 years. The Constitution however states that parents are '. . . free to provide this education in their homes or in schools recognized or established by the State'.[2] In practice most children receive this compulsory education in State-supported schools which are called national schools.

---

[1]For a more complete account of the system of primary education in Ireland see the following:

   (a) *Investment in Education*, Dublin, 1966, pp. 5-7.

   (b) T. J. McElligott, *Education in Ireland*, Dublin, 1967, pp. 1-55.

   (c) *Report of the Council of Education*, (1) *The Function of the Primary School*, (2) *The Curriculum to be pursued in the Primary School from the infant age up to 12 years of age*, Dublin, The Stationery Office, 1955. See especially Chapter XI, 'The Primary School, its Control and Equipment', pp. 216-225.

[2]*Bunreacht na hEireann* (Constitution of Ireland), Article 42(2), Dublin, 1937.

The term national school, however, may be misleading. It has, according to one writer, tended to obscure the fact that national schools are really 'parish schools'.[3] He points out that the national schools

> ... are not owned by the State nor are the national teachers civil servants. Legally they (national teachers) are employed by the managers, even though as happens throughout the country, the State, as the manager's 'agent', directly transmits salaries to them.[4]
>
> The management of the national schools is on a denominational basis, the parish priest being the manager in the case of Catholic schools and the local Protestant clergyman or minister in other cases.[5]

The State pays national teachers. It also provides a grant of not less than two thirds towards the cost of building new schools or improving existing ones, but '... the non-State character of the schools is preserved by insisting on a local contribution to the cost of the building'.[6] McElligott suggests that these two '... basic features of modern Irish primary education—the "managerial system" and the private ownership of the school—can be traced back to its origin under the Board of Education (1831).'[7] Thus, national schools are primary schools which are state-supported but not state-owned. Trained teachers in these schools are referred to as national teachers.

There are three types of primary schools: national schools as defined above; special schools, which are national schools for such categories of pupils as the mentally and physically handicapped; and non-aided primary schools, which receive no support from the state.

Table 3.1 gives the number of each type of primary school in Ireland on 1 February 1964 and also the number of pupils and teachers in these schools. It can be seen that, at that date, there

[3]T. J. McElligott, *op. cit.*, p. 36.
[4]*Ibid.*, p. 36.
[5]*Ibid.*, p. 37. There is one school under Jewish management.
[6]*Ibid.*, p. 37.
[7]*Ibid.*, p. 37.

were almost 5,000 national schools in Ireland and that over 90 per cent of pupils receiving primary education in Ireland attended state-supported national schools.

TABLE 3.1

Primary Schools, Pupils and Teachers in the Republic of Ireland on 1 February, 1964.

Type of School	Number of Schools	Number of Full-time Pupils	Number of Teachers Whole-time	Part-time
National School	4,800	472,124	13,875	—
Special School	41	2,793	189	—
Non-aided Primary School	192	21,151	751	125

Source: Adapted from *Investment in Education*, Table 1.1, p. 4.

In Table 3.2 the numbers of teachers in all national schools in the Republic of Ireland on 30 June 1965 are given.

TABLE 3.2

Teachers in all National Schools in the Republic of Ireland on 30 June, 1965.

Teachers	Trained Men	Women	Untrained Men	Women	Total
Lay	3,749	6,464	18	1,213	11,444
Religious	584	1,812	175	454	3,025
Total	4,333	8,276	193	1,667	14,469

Source: Adapted from Table 19, p. 24, An Roinn Oideachais, *Tuarascail: Tablai Staitistic 1954-65*, Dublin, 1966.

There was a total number of 14,469 teachers in national schools in Ireland. This total number of teachers was subdivided into trained/untrained and lay/religious categories. By far the greatest single category was that of lay, trained teachers, of which there were 10,213, which is over 70 per cent of all teachers in national schools.

National teachers in Ireland are trained in state-aided teacher training colleges,[8] apart from a very small number who are trained according to the Froebel system.[9] In 1965, *Investment in Education* noted that there existed 'six such colleges, one for Catholic men, two for Catholic girls, one for Protestant boys and girls, and two conducted by Catholic teaching orders of brothers for religious'.[10] 'The colleges are under ecclesiastical control and managment, but the selection of students, the appointment and condition of service of professional staff and certain matters of administration (including the amount of the student fee) are subject to the approval of the Minister for Education'.[11] At present there is a two-year full-time course, but university graduates, if admitted, may get certain concessions. 'Candidates selected for training', McElligott points out, 'must obtain honours in Irish and at least a pass in four other subjects in the Leaving Certificate examination'[12]. In fact, to judge by the percentage of students entering with honours in the Leaving Certificate examination, the entrants to the teacher training colleges are academically as highly qualified as the entrants to any faculty in the constituent colleges of the National University.[13]

To summarize, primary education in Ireland is undertaken mainly in national schools. These are parish schools, state-aided but not state-controlled. Ninety per cent of primary students in Ireland are educated in these schools, and 70 per cent of the teachers in them are trained lay teachers.

[8]For a more detailed account of the training of national teachers see: T. J. McElligott, *op. cit.*, pp. 42-45, or *Investment in Education, Annexes and Appendices*, Annexe A, pp. 1-12.

[9]*Investment in Education*, Annexe A, p. 1.

[10]*Ibid.*, p. 1.

[11]*Ibid.*, p.1.

[12]T. J. McElligott, *op. cit.*, p. 42. The requirements for entry to the Training Colleges have been recently changed. The new provisions are contained in Imlitir 3/67 of the Department of Education (March 1967).

[13]*Investment in Education*, p. 120 and p. 127.

The Formal Definition of the Roles of National School Personnel

In this section the roles of the manager, inspector, principal and teacher as formally defined in *Rules for National Schools under the Department of Education* are described.

The duties of the manager of a national school are formulated by the Department of Education as follows: 'The manager . . . is charged with the direct government of the school, the appointment of the teachers, subject to the Minister's approval [i.e. Minister for Education], their removal and the conducting of the necessary correspondence'.[14] It is laid down that managers 'should visit their schools frequently, and should satisfy themselves that the Rules for National Schools are being complied with'.[15] In addition to the manager's responsibility in connection with the building of schools, it is his duty 'to arrange that each school under his charge is adequately furnished and kept in proper structural and decorative condition . . .'[16] Furthermore the Minister 'desires to urge upon the manager the desirability of (a) providing a small library for each school and a small museum of natural objects, furnished, as far as possible, by the pupils themselves; (b) stimulating the school children to greater industry by a system of school prizes . . . .'[17] The Minister for Education has the right to withdraw recognition from a manager in certain circumstances.

A system of inspection of national schools is operated by the Department of Education. 'Inspectors are the agents of the Minister [for Education] and supply him with such local information as he may require for the effective administration of the system.'[18] Inspectors, however, 'are not authorized to decide upon any question affecting a national school . . . and may not give direct orders in a school . . . . They should, however, call the attention of managers and teachers to any rules which appear to them to be infringed . . . .'[19] Other functions of the inspector include (a) paying '. . . frequent

---

[14]*Rules for National Schools under the Department of Education*, Dublin, 1965, p. 12.
[15]*Ibid.*, p. 13.
[16]*Ibid.*, p. 26.
[17]*Ibid.*, p. 14.
[18]*Ibid.*, p. 90.
[19]*Ibid.*, p. 90.

incidental visits to the schools in his district to collaborate in the work of the teachers and to help young teachers and others, who in the inspector's opinion are in need of his assistance and advice'[20] and (b) 'Annual visits . . . to schools for the purpose of general inspections of the work of the teachers'.[21] However, annual general inspections are not obligatory in the case of all teachers.

The duties of the principal teacher in national schools are also given in the *Rules for National Schools*. Rule 123(4) specifies that

> Subject to the authority of the manager the principal teacher is responsible . . . for the discipline of the school generally, the control of the other members of the teaching staff, including the co-ordination and effective supervision of their work, the organization of the school, the keeping of the records of the attendance, the promotion of pupils, the time-table arrangements and their observance, the books used by the pupils, the arrangements in connection with the Free Books Scheme for necessitous children . . . and all other matters connected with the school arrangements in each division.[22]

The principal teacher is also responsible for keeping school records, notably the Roll Book, Report Book and Register. It is also stated that

> corporal punishment should be administered only by the principal teacher or other member of the school staff authorized by the manager for the purpose.[23]

The duties of national teachers, or assistants, are also referred to in the *Rules for National Schools*. Some of these duties are outlined as follows:

[20] *Ibid.*, p. 90.
[21] *Ibid.*, p. 90.
[22] *Ibid.*, p. 72.
[23] *Ibid.*, p. 74. Note that ' . . . co-ordination and effective supervision of their (teachers') work . . .' was included among the specific duties of a principal teacher for the first time in the 1965 edition of *Rules for National Schools*. The possible significance of this will be discussed in chapter IX.

Teachers should pay the strictest attention to the morals and general conduct of their pupils, to the development of a patriotic spirit and outlook and lose no opportunity of inculcating the principles of truth, temperance, unselfishness and politeness and regard for property, whether public or private.[24]

It is also pointed out that 'Teachers should promote, both by precept and example, cleanliness, neatness and decency'.[25] They are required to 'teach each subject in accordance with the requirements of the official programme, using suitable teaching methods, and having regard to the ages, abilities and attainments of the pupils.'[26]

Parents of pupils are not frequently referred to in the *Rules for National Schools*. However, it is stated that parents 'may be given such extracts from the school records regarding the attendance or treatment of their children as might reasonably be expected'.[27] It should be added that 'any person may, with the manager's permission, visit a national school during school hours for the purpose of observing the ordinary working of the school . . .'[28]

Above, then, are briefly outlined the duties prescribed by the Department of Education for the manager, inspector, principal and teacher, or assistant, in national schools in Ireland.

National Schools and Lay National Teachers in Dublin City

The first part of this section gives some information on national schools in Dublin city. The second presents data on some characteristics of the lay teachers who staff these schools, as obtained from the replies of a representative sample of 11 per cent of these teachers to a postal questionnaire.[29]

[24]*Ibid.*, p. 71.
[25]*Ibid.*, p. 71.
[26]*Ibid.*, p. 71.
[27]*Ibid.*, p. 11.
[28]*Ibid.*, p. 11.

[29]The population of the study was defined as all lay national teachers who were members of the Dublin City Branch, I.N.T.O., on 1 October, 1966, excluding principal teachers, teachers in hospital and special schools, and teachers who actually taught outside Co. Dublin. A random sample of 11 per cent of these was selected and sent a postal questionnaire. For further details see Chapter IV and Appendix 3.

1. *National schools in Dublin city.* There were, in June 1965, 289 national schools in Dublin city, staffed by 2,470 national teachers who taught 99,532 pupils. These figures are presented in Table 3.3.

TABLE 3.3

Number of National Schools, Teachers, and Pupils in National Schools in Dublin City on 30 June, 1965

	Catholic	Protestant	Total
Number of Schools	253	36[30]	289
Number of Teachers	2,383	87	2,470
Number of Pupils	96,813	2,719	99,532

National schools can be divided into two groups: (a) schools in which all the teachers are lay; and (b) schools in which at least the principal is a cleric, either a brother or a nun. The former are here referred to as lay schools, the latter as religious schools. Of the 242 Catholic school units in the area covered by Dublin City Branch of the Irish National Teachers' Organization, 53 per cent are lay schools and 47 per cent religious schools. However, the lay schools tend to be small and the religious schools large; almost 70 per cent of the lay schools have less than seven teachers as compared with only 5 per cent of the religious schools.[31] Ninety-five per cent of the religious schools have over six teachers and 16 per cent have over nineteen teachers. Only 1 per cent of the lay schools have over nineteen teachers.[32]

[30] Includes one Jewish school with an enrolment of 108 pupils. Source: An Roinn Oideachais, *Tuarascail, Tablai Staitistic 1964–65,* adapted from Table 5.

[31] Information received from Mr. John Blake, Secretary of the Dublin City Branch, I.N.T.O. Mr Blake sent out a circular to all Catholic school units in the Dublin City Branch, I.N.T.O., in the school year 1966-67, to ascertain the percentage of lay and religious teachers in these schools. This information is set out in table form in Appendix 4.

[32] See Table B.2, Appendix 4.

The great majority of the national teachers in the Catholic schools in Dublin are lay teachers—81 per cent are laymen or women, 12 per cent are nuns and 7 per cent are brothers.[33] These lay teachers work in both lay and religious schools. Among Catholic schools, 57 per cent of lay teachers teach in religious schools and 44 per cent teach in lay schools.[34] Of the sample of Dublin lay teachers taken in this survey, 52 per cent taught in religious schools and 46 per cent in lay schools.[35] It is important to note that the lay teacher who teaches in a religious school cannot become the principal of that school.

Within a national school a teacher may serve in three capacities: principal, vice-principal or special assistant, and assistant. The duties of principals and assistants have been outlined above. Vice-principals or special assistants are usually appointed on the basis of their length of service in the school, there being roughly one vice-principal or special assistant for every four assistants on the staff. While they receive an increased salary vice-principals are not usually made responsible for special functions in the school. In this sample of Dublin lay national teachers, 27 per cent of the men and 14 per cent of the women held the position of vice-principal or special assistant.

2. *Lay Teachers in Dublin.* The number of respondents whose replies were analysed in this survey was 151. This was made up of 48 men (32 per cent) and 103 women (68 per cent). When the percentages of men and women in the sample were compared with those in the Dublin City Branch, Irish National Teachers' Organization (Table 3.4), no significant differences were found. In Ireland as a whole, 33 per cent of lay national teachers are men and 67 per cent are women.

[33]See Table B.3, Appendix 4.
[34]See Table B.4, Appendix 4.
[35]It must be clearly understood that these percentages (52 per cent and 46 per cent) donot refer to the number of lay and religious national schools in Dublin city. In the selection of the sample each lay teacher had an equal chance of being chosen. This meant that in a lay school all the teachers were eligible for selection. The result was that, in terms of schools, lay schools were over-represented in the sample as compared with religious schools. Similarly, in terms of size of school, larger schools were over-represented as compared with smaller schools. This also resulted from the fact that in sampling the individual rather than the schools was the unit of selection.

TABLE 3.4

Number and Percentage*of Men and Women (a) in Dublin City Branch, I.N.T.O. and (b) among Respondents

	Men N	Men %	Women N	Women %	Total N	Total %
Dublin City Branch I.N.T.O.	493	31	1,125	70	1,618	100
Sample	48	32	103	68	151	100

*In this and subsequent tables in the text all percentages are rounded to the nearest whole number and totals are rounded to 100 per cent.

The age of respondents and comparative data on the age structure of all lay national teachers in Ireland are presented in Table 3.5. While the categories used in analysing the ages of respondents do not correspond exactly to those used in the national data they are sufficiently close for general comparisons to be made.

TABLE 3.5

Age of Respondents compared with that of all Lay National Teachers in Ireland

Respondents

Age:	30 or under N	%	31—40 N	%	41—50 N	%	51—60 N	%	Over 60 N	%	Total N	%
Men	24	50	2	4	11	23	8	17	3	6	48	100
Women	39	38	12	12	21	20	26	25	5	5	103	100

Ireland*

Age:	Under 30 N	%	30—39 N	%	40—49 N	%	50—59 N	%	60 or over N	%	Total N	%
Men	991	26	535	14	952	25	993	26	443	11	3,914	100
Women	3,049	38	1,072	13	1,227	15	1,837	23	912	11	7,997	100

*Source: Adapted from *Investment in Education, op. cit.*, Table 4.2, p. 56.

It can be seen from Table 3.5 that while, for all Ireland, 26 per cent of the male lay national teachers were under 30 years of age, 50 per cent of the men in the Dublin sample were 30 years of age or under. The percentage of women teachers in this age group is similar for the Dublin sample and the country as a whole.

It can also be seen from this table that there was an uneven distribution among the various age categories, both for respondents and for all lay national teachers in Ireland. There were proportionately few in the '31—40' age category in the Dublin sample and the '30—40' age category for Ireland as a whole. According to *Investment in Education* this would seem to be a consequence of the restriction on entry to the training colleges during the period 1935 to 1945.[36] This pattern is particularly pronounced in the Dublin sample of men while the high proportion of men under 30 in the Dublin sample has no parallel in the figures for all Ireland.

Concerning the marital status of respondents, 47 per cent of respondents were married, 51 per cent were single, and 2 per cent were widows. A higher percentage of men (58 per cent) than women (42 per cent) were married. This is probably due, in part, to the fact that from 1934 to 1958 women had to retire from teaching when they married and probably also to the demands of family responsibilities on some married women teachers. It was mainly the men and women under thirty who were single. Seventy-nine per cent of the men and 82 per cent of the women under thirty were single while only 4 per cent of the men and 39 per cent of the women over thirty were so.

Some general characteristics of Dublin lay teachers may be summarized as follows: two thirds of these teachers were women, one third men. In terms of age, about 50 per cent of teachers were under forty. However, there were relatively few in the '31—40' age-group, especially in the case of men. Slightly more than half the men and less than half the women were married. However, only a small percentage (20 per cent) of those under thirty years were married.

[36] *Investment in Education,* p. 55.

CHAPTER IV

RESEARCH PROCEDURES USED IN THE STUDY

THE research procedures used in the study are described in this chapter under the following headings: (1) choice of method for gathering data; (2) construction of postal questionnaire; (3) population studied; (4) choice of sample;(5) response waves and the effect of reminders; (6) response rate; and (7) analysis of replies.

Choice of Method for Gathering Data

It was decided to use postal questionnaires to elicit information from teachers on their work. Most textbooks on research methods in sociology point to the danger of inadequate response to this type of questionnaire. Moser, however, says:

> The use of postal questionnaires has been widely condemned for some years on account of the difficulty of securing adequate response. Though serious, this difficulty should not blind one to the merits of the method.[1]

Commenting on a mail survey in which 93 per cent of those contacted replied, Scott says:

> The cost of a mail survey is so low that once this result was known it became essential to ask of every projected interview survey: could the same information be obtained by post?[2]

[1]C. A. Moser, *Survey Methods in Social Investigation*, London, 1958, p. 175.
[2]C. Scott, 'Research on Mail Surveys', p. 144, *Journal of the Royal Statistical Society*—Series A, Vol. 125, Part 2, 1961, pp. 143-205.

The decision to use a postal questionnaire in this study was based on the assumption that a high response rate to it could be obtained. The author's own experience with teachers and his preliminary investigations in the course of which he discussed with teachers their willingness to reply to such questionnaires were the basis for this assumption.

Construction of Postal Questionnaire

To design an adequate postal questionnaire much care must be taken with the formulation of questions. Once questionnaires are dispatched, there is no further possibility of modification or clarification. Accordingly, three drafts of the questionnaire were tested before the final version was adopted.

From the initial discussions with teachers, questions were formulated which dealt with the chief aspects of teaching and the main problems of teachers. A preliminary questionnaire was developed and used in interviews with a number of teachers. It was later modified and given to other teachers. These drafts were used in March and April 1966.

Replies to these questionnaires were examined and in September 1966 a further revision of the questionnaire was prepared. It was tested in a final pilot investigation by sending copies by post to 14 teachers. In addition to completing the questionnaire, each teacher was invited to point out any special difficulties or ambiguities in the questions. After examination of the completed questionnaires, half (seven) of the pilot sample were interviewed; replies they had made were interpreted to them; and they were asked if they thought the interpretation represented their views. In this way further changes were suggested in the format and wording of the questionnaire, and a final draft which appears in Appendix 2 was prepared.[3]

Population Studied

The survey studied lay national teachers in Dublin city. Religious national teachers were excluded as it was thought that, to some extent, their attitudes and problems would

[3] See pp. 154-64.

warrant special investigation. National teachers outside Dublin were also excluded from the survey. It was felt that, initially, an intensive study of a small homogeneous population would be more fruitful. If it proved successful, it could later be extended.

The area covered by the Dublin City Branch of the Irish National Teachers' Organization (I.N.T.O.), is very similar to that of Dublin County Borough (city). It was decided that teachers who were members of the Dublin City Branch, I.N.T.O., should be the population of the study. The committee of this branch made available a full list of all their members on 1 October, 1966; this list was necessary for purposes of sampling. All full members of the I.N.T.O. are lay teachers; hence an advantage of the list was that it did not include religious teachers, who had been excluded from the survey population. It should be noted that 8 per cent of national teachers within the area covered by the Dublin City Branch were not members of the I.N.T.O.[4] These teachers were outside the scope of this study.

After the list of members had been supplied by the branch, it was decided not to investigate certain categories of teachers whose positions, it was thought, warranted special attention. On this basis, principal teachers and teachers in hospital and special schools were excluded. However, a number of these teachers were not identified before sampling, and so appeared in the sample. Their replies were not analysed. Similarly it was found that three teachers were included with school addresses outside Co. Dublin. It is understood that this resulted from a practice whereby teachers who taught outside Co. Dublin, but lived in Dublin city, could apply for membership of the City Branch, I.N.T.O.[5] These teachers were also excluded from the survey.

Sample

As has been said, the population under investigation in this survey was defined as all lay national teachers who were members of the Dublin City Branch of the I.N.T.O. on 1 October 1966, excluding principal teachers, teachers in special

[4]Information supplied by Secretary, Dublin City Branch, I.N.T.O.
[5]Information supplied by the Secretary, Dublin City Branch, I.N.T.O.

schools and hospitals and teachers who actually taught outside
Co. Dublin. From this population a sample of 11 per cent,
numbering 171 teachers, was randomly selected.[6]

Response Waves and the Effect of Reminders

Questionnaires were posted to members of the sample, in
three batches, on 30 November, 1 December and 2 December
1966. An explanatory letter was enclosed stating the purpose of
the survey and asking for the respondent's help. Reminder
letters were sent to those who had not replied on 10 December
1966 and 9 January 1967.

The number of replies received on each day of the survey
may usefully be considered in terms of what C. Scott calls
response waves.[7] A response wave consists of the number of
replies received in response to a particular communication,
whether the first letter or a subsequent reminder. In this
survey there were three response waves. The first consisted of
the number who replied before receiving the first reminder; the
second consisted of those who replied after the first but before
the second reminder; and the third is made up of those who
replied after the second reminder.

The number and percentage of men, women and total in
each wave of replies in this survey are presented in Table 4.1.

TABLE 4·1
Response Waves

Waves	Men		Women		Total		Cumulative Total	
	N	%	N	%	N	%	N	%[8]
First	22	46	45	44	67	44	67	44
Second	21	44	49	48	70	46	137	91
Third	5	10	9	9	14	9	151	100
Total	48	100	103	100	151	100		

This table shows that 44 per cent of the respondents replied
before receiving the first reminder. This first wave extended
over ten days, after which the first reminder was dispatched.

[6]For further details of sampling procedure see Appendix 3, pp. 165-6.
[7]C. Scott, *op. cit.*, pp. 160-164.
[8]The percentage referred to here is the percentage of all who actually replied.

This reminder elicited the response of a further 46 per cent. A second reminder, dispatched almost a month later, elicited the remaining 9 per cent of responses. It can also be seen from this table that there was little difference between the percentages of men and women respondents in each response wave.

Response

Of the 171 questionnaires sent out, 161 were returned completed, one was returned because the addressee had retired from teaching and gone abroad, another was returned uncompleted and without comment. No replies were received from 8 teachers (7 women and 1 man). Of the 161 who replied 9 were found to be principal teachers and one had retired from teaching. Their replies were not analysed. Accordingly, 151 was the actual number of replies on which the final analysis was based. The response rate was 94 per cent, which is unusually high for a postal survey.

Analysis of Replies

As the questionnaires were returned their date of arrival was recorded and any omissions or special points of interest were noted.[9]

Coding of replies to questions for which precoded response categories were used gave little difficulty. However, considerable difficulty was experienced with open-ended questions such as numbers 8 and 9.[10] This was overcome by examining closely the replies of thirty respondents and forming categories of response based on them. These categories were changed three times before the final categories were adopted.

When coding was complete, the author punched the coded information on to I.B.M. 5081 cards. Eighty items of information were extracted from each questionnaire. Thus one punched card was sufficient to take all the required information from a single questionnaire. Final data-processing was done on the University College, Dublin, I.B.M. 1620 computer using the WARDEN[11] and CAST[12] programme.

[9]Six respondents replied in Irish. Their replies were translated into English before coding.

[10]See Appendix 2, pp. 157-8.

[11]This was written by Rev. Professor Ingram, University College, Dublin, in 1966.

[12]Cross and Simple Tabulation Program, 60.146, 1620 General Program Library, written by Howard Givner, 1964.

CHAPTER V

SOCIAL ORIGINS OF TEACHERS

In this chapter results of the study of the social origins of respondents are presented. A knowledge of the social origins of the members of any profession or occupation helps to understand their position in society by identifying the environmental and cultural areas from which they came. A knowledge of the social origins of teachers helps not only to do this, but also to understand the teacher-pupil and teacher-parent relationship especially if pupils and parents come from a different social background to the teacher.[1]

In the first two sections of this chapter the social origins of teachers are identified in terms of the social groups[2] and geographical areas[3] from which they originated. In the third section the social origins of teachers in Dublin city are compared with those of their pupils. Although only a crude comparison is possible, it is hoped that it will be a first step in examining the extent to which differences in social origins cause problems of communication between teachers and pupils. The relationship between social origins and parent-teacher relations is discussed in Chapter VII.

Social Group Origin of Respondents

The social group origin of respondents was investigated by asking respondents to state the occupations of their fathers (question 22). In the analysis of replies to this question four occupational categories were used:

[1]See Chapter II, pp. 17-19.
[2]The 'Social group origin' of respondents means the occupational category to which their fathers belong. Social group may be taken as roughly synonymous with social class.
[3]See Chapter II, p. 21.

1. Farmer (Social group O).[4]
2. Professional and employer-managerial (Social groups 2 to 5).
3. Intermediate non-manual and other non-manual (Social groups 6 and 7).
4. Manual (Social groups 8, 9 and 10).

The occupations of the fathers of respondents are presented in Table 5.1, using these four categories. It can be seen that a higher percentage of teachers had fathers in the category 'farmer' than in any other occupational category. Thirty-four per cent of the respondents had fathers who were in the 'farmer' category and 32 per cent in the 'professional and employer managerial' category. It is of interest to note that 60 per cent of those in this latter category had fathers who were national teachers, which amounts to 20 per cent of all the respondents. It can be seen from the table that relatively few of the teachers came from 'intermediate and other non-manual' (18 per cent) or from 'manual' (10 per cent) occupational categories.

TABLE 5.1

The Occupation by Social Category of Fathers of Respondents

Father's Occupational Category	Men		Women		Total	
	N	%	N	%	N	%
Farmer	13	27	39	38	52	34
Professional & employer-managerial	13	27	35	34	48	32
Intermediate & other non-manual	8	17	19	19	27	18
Manual	9	19	6	6	15	10
Other	3	6	1	1	4	3
No reply	2	4	3	3	5	3
Total	48	100	103	100	151	100

[4]The social groups and code numbers are based on those used in the Census of Population of Ireland 1961. See *Census of Population of Ireland 1961*, Vol. III. Appendix C, Dublin, 1963.

There appear to be some differences in the social background of men and women teachers. Women more frequently than men had fathers in professional, managerial and other non-manual occupations, while men more frequently had fathers in manual occupations. It will be remembered from Chapter II that this tendency for male teachers to come from a lower class origin than women teachers also prevails in England and Wales and in the United States.[5]

It is probable that national teaching in Ireland is an avenue for upward social mobility, as teaching is in England and the United States. Teachers whose fathers were in the 'manual', 'intermediate and other non-manual' categories, and the majority from the 'farmer' category[6] may be considered upwardly mobile. However, fewer Irish teachers had fathers who worked in manual occupations (10 per cent) than had teachers in England and the United States (30 to 40 per cent).

To investigate the extent to which teachers were representative of all social groups, Table 5.2 was prepared. This table

TABLE 5.2

Percentage Distribution of a, b, c, & d (as defined below) by Father's Occupational Category, compared with the percentage distribution of these categories in the Basic Population

Occupational Category	Respondents in this survey %	Lay students entering Tr. Cols. (1963) %	Leaving Cert Candidates (1963) %	University entrants (1963) %	Basic Population %
Farmers	34	33	20	20	25
Professional, employer, managerial, intermediate & other non-manual	50	35	54	65	30
Manual	10	10	11	9	40
Other	3	3	4	2	—
No information	3	19	11	4	5
Total	100	100	100	100	100

[5]See Chapter II, p. 18.
[6]See Table A.76, Appendix 1. The majority of fathers in the 'farmer' category came from small farm regions.

shows the percentage of the fathers of (a) respondents, (b) lay students entering training colleges (1963),[7] (c) leaving certificate candidates (1963), and (d) university entrants (1963), in three occupational categories compared with the percentage of each category in the basic population (1961).[8]

The table shows that a higher proportion of teachers surveyed (34 per cent) came from farming backgrounds than might have been expected on the basis of the proportion of leaving certificate candidates who were sons of farmers (20 per cent), and from the proportion of farmers in the basic population (25 per cent). It can also be seen from this table that farmers, professional and white collar workers constituted 55 per cent of the basic population, yet supplied 84 per cent of the teachers in the survey. Manual workers constituted 40 per cent of the population but supplied only 10 per cent of these teachers.

Investment in Education has interpreted this '. . . traditional attachment of certain social groups to teaching as a career',[9] in terms of the different educational and economic opportunities open to each social group. It is however possible that changes in the access of different social groups to these opportunities may also cause changes in the social origins of teachers.

Geographical Origin of Respondents

Respondents were asked to state their county of birth (question 23). The results obtained from an analysis of replies to this question are given in Table 5.3 and are compared with similar information for entrants to training colleges (1963) and for the total population (1961). Twenty-five per cent of the total population lived in Dublin, yet only 12 per cent of the male respondents and 4 per cent of the female respondents were born there. Only 3 per cent of the lay entrants to training colleges in 1963 had their homes in Dublin. A much higher proportion of respondents and entrants to training colleges came from counties Galway, Mayo, Clare and Kerry in comparison

---

[7] *Investment in Education, Annexes and Appendices, op. cit.,* p. 6.

[8] Source of figures for (c), (d), and basic population: *Investment in Education, op. cit.,* p.172.

[9] *Investment in Education, Annexes and Appendices. op. cit.,* p. 7.

with the proportion of the total population living in these counties. Thus national teachers tended not only to come from certain social groups but also from certain geographical areas.

TABLE 5.3

Location of Home of Respondents' Parents and of Lay Entrants to Training Colleges (1963) compared with Percentage Distribution of Total Population (1961)

| Location of Parents' Home | Respondents | | Entrants to Training Colleges* | | Total Population |
| | Men | Women | Men | Women | |
	%	%	%	%	%
Dublin (City & County)	12	4	3	3	25
Rest of Leinster	12	11	10	18	22
Clare/Kerry	21	22	22	16	7
Rest of Munster	35	15	25	21	23
Galway/Mayo	10	25	20	26	9
Rest of Connaught	—	8	4	6	5
Donegal/Cavan/Monaghan	4	16	17	9	8
U.S.A.	4	—	—	—	—
Total (%)	100	100	100	100	100
Total N	48	103	131	289	2,818,341

*Source: *Investment in Education, Annexes and Appendices*, p. 8.

It is of interest to note that respondents who came from Munster, from Galway and Mayo, and from Leinster (apart from Dublin) tended more frequently to have farming backgrounds than teachers from other areas.[10] Respondents from Dublin and from the northern counties tended to originate from middle-class groups or white collar worker backgrounds. Dublin and the rest of Leinster also accounted for proportionately more respondents from working-class backgrounds than other areas. The numbers involved, however, are too small to make generalizations possible.

[10]See Table A.76, Appendix 1.

Social Origins of Teachers and Pupils

Sociologists have suggested that differences between the social origins of teachers and their pupils may cause difficulties in communication.[11] This problem was not specifically investigated in this study. However, an initial step, which is attempted in this section, is to identify whether these differences in social origins do in fact exist.

There are two limitations to the comparisons made between the social origins of national teachers and their pupils in Dublin city. Firstly, teachers were asked to identify the type of area from which the majority of their pupils came and in some instances this may have been difficult to do precisely. Secondly, since teachers were asked to identify the type of area rather than the social group[12] from which the majority of their pupils came, it must be noted that there may not always exist a perfect relationship between a 'type of area' and the social group of people who live there.

Despite these limitations, and the crudity of the measure, this analysis is still felt to be valuable, because even allowing for inaccuracies the differences between the social origins of teachers and their pupils were found to be great.

All the pupils of the respondents came from Dublin city. To identify the type of area in the city from which they came, respondents were asked (question 24) to indicate whether the majority of their pupils came from:

1. Poor city centre area
2. Corporation pre-1939 estate
3. Corporation post-1944 estate, or
4. Privately owned housing.

The type of area from which the majority of the pupils taught by respondents came is set out in Table 5.4.

---

[11]See Chapter II, pp. 17-18.

[12]The type of area rather than the social class categories of 'upper class', 'upper middle class', 'lower middle class' and 'lower class' were used because of the difficulty respondents in the pilot survey had in interpreting these latter categories.

TABLE 5.4

Type of Area from which the Majority of the Pupils taught by Respondents came

Type of Area	Men N	Men %	Women N	Women %	Total N	Total %
Poor city centre area	10	21	14	14	24	16
Corporation pre-1939 estate	6	13	9	9	15	10
Corporation post-1944 estate	18	38	42	41	60	40
Privately owned housing	14	29	37	36	51	34
Don't know	—	—	1	1	1	1
Total	48	100	103	100	151	100

Sixteen per cent of respondents taught classes in which the majority of the pupils came from poor city centre areas, while 50 per cent taught classes in which the majority of the pupils came from corporation housing estates. In these districts the majority of the fathers of families are usually in manual or service employment, and few in 'intermediate non-manual' employment. Thus about 66 per cent of the respondents taught classes in which the majority of pupils were the children of manual and service workers. The percentage of teachers coming from a similar origin was between 10 per cent[13] and 28 per cent.[14]

As stated above, all the pupils taught by respondents came from Dublin city. Only 7 per cent of the respondents came from Dublin, and the majority of teachers came from Munster and Connaught. The extent to which there are significant cultural differences between Munster, Connaught and Dublin was not investigated and so the educational effects of the above situation are not known. It is clear, however, that many children of manual workers in Dublin are being taught by teachers whose social class and geographical origins are different from those of their pupils.

[13]Includes respondents with fathers in occupational categories: other non-manual, skilled, semi-skilled and unskilled manual workers. Cf. Table 5.1, p. 39.

[14]Includes all the above and also respondents with fathers in the intermediate non-manual category.

CHAPTER VI

THE ROLE OF THE TEACHER

IN this chapter the research findings on the role definition and role-set of the teacher are discussed separately, and an attempt will be made at the end of the chapter to integrate them.

Role Definition

By role definition is meant the set of expectations applied to the incumbents of a particular position. Role definers are those who specify what the set of expectations is. In this study, the particular position investigated was that of lay national teacher in Dublin city and the role definers were taken to be those teachers themselves. This aspect of the study, then, attempted to discover what teachers felt were the central and the marginal obligations in teaching.

1. *Areas of Teacher Behaviour Chosen for Investigation.* Having made preliminary investigations and considered the relevant literature; the author selected for study the following four areas of teacher behaviour:

 (i) The religious, moral and social development of pupils
 (ii) The academic development of pupils
 (iii) The establishment of contact with parents and the wider community, and
 (iv) Participation in extra-curricular activities.

To investigate the degree to which teachers felt these areas were central or marginal obligations in teaching a role definition instrument (RDI)[1] was developed in connection with the questionnaire. In question 7 a series of items was presented in

---

[1]See M. Gross, W. S. Mason, and A. W. McEachern, *op. cit.*, p. 331. The general format of the RDI resembles that used by Gross in his school superintendency study.

45

random order, each of which specified an activity in which teachers might possibly be expected to engage. Each of these activities was related to one of the four areas of teacher behaviour chosen for investigation. For example, the area of teacher behaviour, 'the establishment of contact with parents and the wider community,' was investigated through the items:

—Invite parents of difficult pupils to come and see him.
—Send reports on pupils' progress to parents.
—Organize parent-teacher meetings.
—Live in the parish he teaches in.

Altogether there were 17 such items. Respondents were asked to reply to each one by indicating how obligatory they thought the activity mentioned in the item should be on teachers. In answering, they had a choice of five levels of obligation:

1. Absolutely must
2. Preferably should
3. May or may not
4. Preferably should not
5. Absolutely should not.

2. *Analysis of Replies.* In the case of each item in the RDI, the number replying in each response category was counted, as the following example shows:—

Obligation

	Absolutely must	Preferably should	May or may not	Preferably should not	Absolutely should not
Ensure that pupils perform their religious duties	34	69	19	17	9

The actual numbers in each category were then reckoned as percentages of all who replied to that item. Separate, but similar calculations were made for men, women and the total of all respondents. Table 6.1 gives the results thus calculated for the item 'ensure that pupils perform their religious duties'. Similar tables were prepared for each item in the R.D.I. and are given in Appendix 1.[2]

²See Tables A.1 to A.17, Appendix 1.

TABLE 6.1

Obligation felt by Respondents to ensure that Pupils perform Religious Duties

Obligation	Men		Women		Total	
	N	%	N	%	N	%
Absolutely must	12	25	22	21	34	23
Preferably should	21	44	48	47	69	46
May or may not	3	6	16	16	19	13
Preferably should not	8	17	9	9	17	11
Absolutely should not	3	6	6	6	9	6
Does not apply to me	—	—	1	1	1	1
No reply	1	2	1	1	2	1
Total	48	100	103	100	151	100

Replies on the RDI were summarized by calculation of the *mean* and *variance* for each item. The response categories— 'absolutely must', 'preferably should', 'may or may not', 'preferably should not' and 'absolutely should not'—were allotted weightings of 1, 2, 3, 4 and 5 respectively. Thus 1 is the weighting of 'absolutely must' while 5 is that of 'absolutely should not'. The number of responses in each category was multiplied by the appropriate numerical weighting; the products were added and the result divided by the total number who replied to the item. The result of this calculation is the mean $\bar{X}$, which is a measure of the overall direction and intensity of the obligation felt. All means must range between 1 and 5—the nearer the mean is to 1 the more obligatory the activity mentioned in the item is felt to be. In addition to the mean, the variance (V) for each item was calculated. The variance indicates the amount of agreement among respondents on the extent of the obligation, and the smaller the variance the greater the agreement (consensus).

The following example shows how the mean was calculated:

C

Obligation

	Absolutely must	*Preferably should*	*May or may not*	*Preferably should not*	*Absolutely should not*
Ensure that pupils perform their religious duties	34×1	$+\quad 69 \times 2$	$+\quad 19 \times 3$	$+\quad 17 \times 4$	$+\quad 9 \times 5 =$

$$\frac{342}{148} = 2 \cdot 3$$

Mean $(\bar{X})$ $= 2 \cdot 3$
Variance (V) $= 1 \cdot 2$

This procedure provided a method of summarizing results on the RDI and accordingly Table 6.2 was prepared. It shows the mean $(\bar{X})$ and variance (V) of scores on each item for men, women and the total number of respondents. Significant differences, at the 5 per cent level, in mean and variance of men and women are also shown. The items are listed in Table 6.2 in rank order according to the size of the total mean. The reader may see from this table the degree to which respondents felt each activity was obligatory for teachers.

3. *Discussion of Results.* In the following discussion of results the RDI items will be classified by the area of teacher behaviour to which they referred.

(i) *Religious, moral and social development of pupils.* The degree to which respondents felt obliged to ensure the religious, moral and social development of their pupils was investigated through their replies to seven items. These items were:

—Give good example to pupils by his behaviour in school
—Develop the moral character of his pupils
—Try to ensure that pupils grow up good Christians
—Help pupils become good members of society
—Give good example to pupils outside school
—Develop in the pupils a love of Ireland
—Ensure that pupils perform their religious duties.

TABLE 6.2

Mean ($\bar{X}$) and Variance (V) of Expectations of Men, Women and Total on each item of Role Definition Instrument[3]

Rank Order	Items		Men	Women	Significant Differences (Men & Women)	Total
1	Give good example to pupils by his behaviour in school	$\bar{X}$	1·1	1·1	—	1·1
		V	0·1	0·1	—	0·1
1	Train pupils to think	$\bar{X}$	1·2	1·1	—	1·1
		V	0·2	0·1	—	0·1
3	Develop the moral character of his pupils	$\bar{X}$	1·3	1·2	—	1·2
		V	0·2	0·2	—	0·2
3	Try to ensure that pupils grow up good Christians	$\bar{X}$	1·3	1·1	Sig.	1·2
		V	0·1	0·2	—	0·2
3	Help pupils become good members of society	$\bar{X}$	1·2	1·2	—	1·2
		V	0·2	0·2	—	0·2
6	Give good example to pupils by his behaviour outside school	$\bar{X}$	1·6	1·4	—	1·5
		V	0·9	0·4	Sig.	0·6
6	Develop in the pupils a love of Ireland	$\bar{X}$	1·5	1·6	—	1·5
		V	0·2	0·4	—	0·3
8	Invite parents of difficult pupils to come and see him	$\bar{X}$	1·7	1·6	—	1·6
		V	0·9	0·6	Sig.	0·7
9	Give individual attention to backward children	$\bar{X}$	2·0	1·5	Sig.	1·7
		V	1·4	0·5	Sig.	0·8
10	Teach the prescribed programme	$\bar{X}$	2·2	1·8	Sig.	1·9
		V	0·7	0·6	—	0·7
11	Send reports on pupils' progress to parents	$\bar{X}$	2·0	2·2	—	2·1
		V	0·5	0·7	—	0·6
12	Ensure that pupils perform their religious duties	$\bar{X}$	2·3	2·3	—	2·3
		V	1·4	0·9	Sig.	1·2
13	Extend his teaching beyond the prescribed programme	$\bar{X}$	2·5	2·4	—	2·5
		V	1·4	1·0	Sig.	1·2
14	Give special attention to very bright pupils	$\bar{X}$	2·9	2·7	—	2·8
		V	1·4	1·4	—	1·4
15	Organize games for pupils after school	$\bar{X}$	2·7	3·5	Sig.	3·2
		V	0·9	0·8	—	0·8
16	Organize parent-teacher meetings	$\bar{X}$	3·6	3·3	—	3·4
		V	1·4	1·2	—	1·3
17	Live in the parish he teaches in	$\bar{X}$	3·4	3·6	—	3·5
		V	1·0	1·0	—	1·0

[3]A series of detailed tables, like 6.1 above, for each item in the RDI is given in Appendix 1, Tables A.1 to A.17. The standard deviation and standard error of each mean are given in Appendix 1, Table A.24.

It can be seen from Table 6.2 that all these items, except the last, ranked at the top of the list. This indicates that ensuring the religious, moral and social development of pupils was felt by teachers to be the most obligatory form of behaviour for them. Each of these items will now be discussed in detail.

—Give good example to pupils by his behaviour in school, Rank 1. This was one of the two items on which teachers put most emphasis, a mean score of 1·1 indicating how close to 'absolutely must' it was felt to be by all respondents. The very low variance (0·1) shows the great degree of consensus among respondents on this item. Agreement between men and women is shown by the identical scores for each.

—Develop the moral character of his pupils, Rank 3. This item also has a very low mean and variance, indicating that all respondents felt it embodied a great obligation on teachers. Again there were no significant differences between the scores of men and women.

—Try to ensure that pupils grow up good Christians, Rank 3. The total mean of 1·2 shows that all respondents felt this item embodied a great obligation. A significant difference was found between the mean scores of men (1·3) and women (1·1) on this item, indicating that women felt more that this item was obligatory on teachers than did men.

—Help pupils become good members of society, Rank 3. This was felt to be highly obligatory by all respondents as the mean of 1·2 indicates. No significant differences were found between the scores of men and women on this item.

—Give good example to pupils by his behaviour outside school, Rank 6. The overall mean score on this item is 1·5 indicating an obligation felt by respondents to lie halfway between 'absolutely should' and 'preferably should'. The men's score of 1·6 was higher than that of the women, 1·4, but not significantly so. There was, however, a significant difference between the variances for men (0·9) and women (0·4), indicating a significantly wider range of opinions among men than among women on the obligations of teachers in relation to this item.

—Develop in the pupils a love of Ireland, Rank 6. An overall mean score of 1·5 indicates that this is an obligation felt to lie between 'absolutely must' and 'preferably should'. There were no significant differences between the opinions of men and women on this item.

—Ensure that pupils perform their religious duties, Rank 12. The overall mean for this item is 2·3, indicating that the obligation felt by teachers concerning this item was between 'preferably should' and 'may or may not', but more inclined towards the former. The mean score was the same for men and women. There was a significant difference in the variance, however, which indicated a wider range of opinion among men than among women on this item.

The results of an analysis of the items under 'religious, moral and social development of pupils' show therefore that teachers felt this to be one of their most important obligations. It would appear that they thought it should be done by good example but did not feel that their obligations in this sphere extended to ensuring the performance of religious duties. Two items referred to giving good example, of which 'giving good example in school' was ranked joint first, and 'giving good example outside school' joint third. Giving good example is an unspecific and diffuse activity, and the importance which these teachers placed on it supports the idea of teaching as an unspecific, unspecialized, wide-ranging occupation. The importance placed on the giving of good example outside school indicates that respondents regarded teaching as a job which is 'never finished'. The high commitment of teachers to the religious, moral and social development of pupils shows that they perceived their job as having important functions other than teaching actual subject matter.

(ii) *Intellectual and academic development of pupils*. The degree to which respondents felt obliged to ensure the intellectual and academic development of their pupils was investigated through their replies to five items:

—Train pupils to think
—Give individual attention to backward children
—Teach the prescribed programme
—Extend his teaching beyond the prescribed programme
—Give special attention to very bright pupils.

It can be seen from Table 6.2 that, excepting 'training pupils to think' which was ranked joint first, all the other items fell into the latter half of the list, ranking from ninth to fourteenth. The ranking of 'teach the prescribed programme' at tenth may be of particular interest.

—Train pupils to think, Rank 1. The mean on this item is very low(1·1), showing the high value put on the intellectual development of pupils. There were no significant differences between the views of men and women on this item.

—Give individual attention to backward children, Rank 9. The total mean of 1·7 shows this to be felt as a considerable obligation. However, there is a significant difference between the mean scores of men (2·0) and women (1·5) on this item, indicating that women felt more that teachers were obliged to give special attention to backward children than did men.

—Teach the prescribed programme, Rank 10. The overall mean score of 1·9 appears rather high. One might expect that teaching the prescribed programme would be seen as an 'absolutely must' by most teachers. However, in view of the dissatisfaction expressed with the curriculum[4] it could be that this score reflects a lack of enthusiasm for the content of the prescribed programme rather than a feeling that teaching it is an unimportant part of a teacher's work. There was a significant difference between the mean scores of men (2·2) and women (1·8), indicating that the men saw this item as less obligatory than did women.

—Extend his teaching beyond the prescribed programme, Rank 13. The overall mean of 2·5 indicates that some obligation to do this was felt.

—Give special attention to very bright pupils, Rank 14. The total mean of 2·8 shows that this is one of the items which teachers felt to be close to the 'may or may not' category.

It would therefore appear that respondents felt a strong obligation to develop their pupils intellectually. They did not feel, however, that teachers were absolutely bound to do this through the prescribed programme. They thought that there was even less of an obligation on teachers to extend their

[4]See Chapter VIII, pp. 94-5 and pp. 102-3.

teaching beyond the prescribed programme. It appeared that teachers felt much more inclined towards the diffuse and non-specific activity of teaching their pupils to think, than towards the specific activity of teaching the prescribed programme.

Teachers felt that they 'preferably should' help backward children but 'may or may not' help bright students. It should be noted that respondents were asked to state what obligations they felt were on teachers to do certain things having regard to the current conditions in Dublin, and the large size of classes and lack of teaching aids, both of which were major sources of dissatisfaction for teachers,[5] may constitute unfavourable conditions within which to give special help to either backward or bright students.

(iii) *Establish contact with parents and the wider community.* Replies on four items were used as indicators of the degree of obligation respondents felt was on teachers to establish contact with parents and the wider community. These were:

—Invite parents of difficult pupils to come and see him
—Send reports on pupils' progress to parents
—Organize parent-teacher meetings
—Live in the parish he teaches in.

Table 6.2 shows that while the first of these items ranks eighth and the second eleventh, the last two rank sixteenth and seventeenth at the bottom of the list.

—Invite parents of difficult pupils to come and see him, Rank 8. The overall mean score of 1.6 on this item shows that it was felt to be quite strongly obligatory. It is also interesting that there was a significant difference between the variance of men (0·9) and women (0·6) which indicates that there was more agreement among women than men on this item.

—Send reports on pupils' progress to parents, Rank 11. The overall mean of 2·1 indicates that respondents felt that this obligation was at the 'preferably should' level. There were no significant differences between the mean scores or variances of men and women.

[5] See Chapter VIII.

—Organize parent-teacher meetings, Rank 16. The mean of 3·4 on this item shows that the overall obligation was felt to lie between 'may or may not' and 'preferably should not'. The relatively large variance scores for both men (1·4) and women (1·2) indicate the wide variation of responses to this item.

—Live in the parish he teaches in, Rank 17. The overall mean score of 3·5 on this item is the highest of any of the 17 role-definition items, indicating that respondents felt this item to be least obligatory on teachers. It is also interesting that women scored higher than men on this item, one of the few for which this was so.

Respondents did not feel that teachers were obliged to establish contact with parents and the wider community, except with parents of difficult pupils. They felt that teachers were obliged to invite parents of difficult pupils to come to see them, but that teachers should not necessarily have to organize parent-teacher associations or live in the parish in which they taught. These facts will be further discussed in the following chapter on parent-teacher relations.

(iv) *Extra-curricular activities*. The degree to which teachers felt obliged to participate in extra-curricular activities was investigated by inquiring whether or not they felt obliged to organize games for pupils after school. It can be seen from Table 6.2 that this item ranked fifteenth, third from the bottom of the list. The overall mean of 3·2 shows that it was almost in the 'may or may not' category. The difference between the mean for men (2·7) and that for women (3·5) is significant, and may be explained by the fact that in most boys' schools in Dublin city games are arranged by teachers for pupils after school hours.

4. *Summary of the Role Definition of the Teacher*. Perhaps the most striking thing about the responses to the role-definition instrument (RDI) is the extent to which unspecific, diffuse obligations are dominant. The first seven items in Table 6.2 are all concerned with these kinds of activities. The emphasis is on broad moral, religious and intellectual development of

pupils and the giving of good example in school was felt to be considerably more important than teaching the prescribed programme. Accordingly, it would appear that respondents saw teaching not as a specific activity involving the imparting of knowledge but as an activity where every aspect of the teacher's behaviour is relevant. *Rules for National Schools* says that

> Teachers should pay the strictest attention to the morals and general conduct of their pupils, to the development of a patriotic spirit and outlook and lose no opportunity of inculcating the principles of truth, temperance, unselfishness and politeness and regard for property, whether public or private.[6]

It seems that respondents would accept these injunctions as an outline of priorities in a teacher's work.

Another aspect of the responses to the RDI is the extent to which pupil-centred items were felt to be more obligatory than others. Especially relevant is the clear indication that respondents felt that teachers were not strongly obliged to contact parents, send reports on pupils' progress to them, or organize meetings with them. This topic will be discussed again in Chapters VII and IX.

There were few differences between the scores of men and women on the RDI. Only on the mean scores of four of the seventeen items were there significant sex differences. On three of these four items, men felt less obliged than did women. These items were: 'ensure that pupils grow up good Christians', 'give individual attention to backward children', and 'teach the prescribed programme'. Men felt that teachers were more obliged to organize games for pupils outside school.

There were significant differences in the variances of men and women on five of the RDI items. On each of these, the variance of men was significantly higher than that of women, indicating that on these items there was less agreement among men than among women. These items were concerned with giving good example outside school, giving individual attention to back-

---

[6]*Rules for National Schools under the Department of Education*, p. 71.

ward children, ensuring the performance of religious duties, extending teaching beyond the prescribed programme and inviting parents of difficult pupils to come and see the teacher. This finding would need further investigation, especially in terms of the age difference of respondents, and the difference in the types of school in which they taught before any definite interpretation could be given to it.

Finally, a note on the RDI itself. It appears that an instrument of this kind is efficient in obtaining information on what are felt to be the role obligations of the incumbents of a position. The calculation of the mean and variance for each item allows a useful summary of results to be made. The instrument used here was short and could usefully be extended to include a wider range of activities.

Role-set

In the investigation of the role-set of the teacher it was decided to examine the relationships of the teacher (focal position) with the following counter positions: parent, pupil, inspector, colleague, principal and manager. There are two aspects to this study of role-set. The first investigates the degree to which each counter position was felt by teachers to influence their work. The second studies the expectations which teachers felt that counter positions held of them.

The following consideration should be held in mind throughout this chapter: there may be a discrepancy between what teachers feel incumbents of counter positions expect of them and what these incumbents in fact expect. However, teachers may attempt to fulfil what they themselves perceive as expected of them, whether or not what they do is actually expected.

1. *Influence of various counter positions.* This section investigates the degree to which each counter position was felt by teachers to influence their work. Question 5 was included in the questionnaire for this purpose. The list of counter positions chosen for investigation was presented to each teacher who was asked to mark the degree of influence the incumbents of each position had on his work.[7] Four response categories were provided:

1. Very much
2. To some extent
3. Slightly
4. Not at all.

The number of replies in each category was counted. In the case of the counter position 'colleague' the following figures were obtained:—

	Influence			
	Very much	*To some extent*	*Slightly*	*Not at all*
Colleague	21	47	44	36

To summarize this data the mean and variance were calculated.[8] The mean for this counter position was 2·6 and the variance 1·0. Similar calculations were made for each of the counter positions and the results are given in Table 6.3. The full tables from which these summary figures were calculated together with the standard deviation and standard error of each mean are given in Appendix 1.[9]

From Table 6.3 it can be observed that only one of the counter positions has a mean score of less than 2. This is the position of pupil which has a score of 1·4, indicating that respondents felt that they were most influenced in their work by the attitudes of their pupils. This is especially interesting in view of the role definition findings which showed the importance for teachers of pupil-centred activities.

In rank order of degree of influence, inspector comes second (2·3), principal third (2·5), colleagues fourth (2·6), parents

[7]It is possible that, had a question been asked specifying different aspects of a teachers' role rather than the general question of influence on work, teachers might have indicated that incumbents of various counter positions had differential influence in each of these areas.

[8]The procedures explained on pp. 47–8 were used. Weightings of 1, 2, 3, 4 were given to the response categories, 'very much', 'to some extent', 'slightly', and 'not at all', respectively.

[9]Tables A.18 to A.23. Standard deviations are in Table A.24, Appendix 1.

TABLE 6.3

Degree of Influence Respondents felt is Exercised on their work by Incumbents of Counter Positions as indicated by Mean ($\bar{X}$) and Variance (V) for each Counter Position

Rank Order	Counter positions		Men	Women	Significant Differences	Total
1	Pupils	$\bar{X}$	1·7	1·3	Sig.	1·4
		V	0·6	0·5	—	0·6
2	Inspector	$\bar{X}$	2·4	2·2	—	2·3
		V	0·8	0·6	—	0·7
3	Principal	$\bar{X}$	2·6	2·4	—	2·5
		V	0·6	0·9	Sig.	0·8
4	Colleagues	$\bar{X}$	2·5	2·7	—	2·6
		V	0·9	1·0	—	1·0
5	Parents	$\bar{X}$	3·0	2·8	—	2·8
		V	0·5	0·9	Sig.	0·9
6	Manager	$\bar{X}$	3·4	3·4	—	3·4
		V	0·6	0·7	—	0·7

fifth (2·8) and manager sixth (3·4). It is interesting that the inspector should be felt to have more influence than the principal or colleagues, although the differences are small. The manager appears to have less influence than any other counter position; his influence was felt to be approximately half-way between 'slightly' and 'not at all'.

There were few significant differences between the scores of men and women. The only significant difference in mean score was in the case of 'pupils' where men scored 1·7 and women 1·3 indicating that women felt more that their work was influenced by pupils than did men. Significant differences in variance were found for 'principal' and 'parents'. In each case the variance for women was higher indicating that there was less agreement on the influence of principal and parents among women than among men.

Thus it would appear that respondents were mainly influenced in their work by their pupils and least of all by the school manager.

2. *What respondents consider counter position incumbents expect of them.* The second part of the investigation of the role-set of the teacher consisted of a study of what expectations teachers felt counter position incumbents held for them. It was decided to seek this information through an open-ended question since it proved impossible to develop a satisfactory pre-coded question. Respondents were asked to indicate what they thought was chiefly expected from them as teachers by parents, colleagues, pupils, inspector, manager and principal (question 8).

In coding the replies, nine categories were developed. These were:

—Kindness/Understanding/Good example/Character formation
—Teach prescribed programme and Kindness etc. (as in previous category)
—Teach prescribed programme
—Examination success
—Conscientious work
—Conformity to rules/Maintain status quo
—Loyalty/Co-operation
—Religious and moral development of pupils
—Not interested/Little contact/No expectations/Do not know.

Using these coding categories, Table 6.4 presents a summary of the respondents' perception of what was chiefly expected of them by the incumbents of the six counter positions. These expectations are discussed below.

(*i*) *Pupils:* Seventy-one per cent of the respondents stated that pupils expected such characteristics as kindness, understanding, fairness and good example from them.[10] This was the view of a higher percentage of women (77 per cent) than men (60 per cent).

(*ii*) *Inspector:* Thirty-nine per cent of the respondents felt that the inspector expected them to teach the prescribed pro-

[10]Figure obtained by addition of first two categories.

TABLE 6.4

Summary of Respondents' Perception of what was chiefly expected of them by Incumbents of Counter Positions[11]

Chief Expectations	Pupils	Counter Positions (Percentage)			Parents	Manager
		Inspector	Principal	Colleagues		
Kindness/Under standing/Good Example/Character formation	44	1	—	—	9	—
Teach prescribed programme and Kindness etc.	27	14	16	4	38	13
Teach prescribed programme	2	25	7	9	13	1
Examination success	1	1	3	—	13	1
Conscientious work	—	19	34	—	5	18
Conform to rules/ maintain status quo	—	12	19	—	—	13
Loyalty/ Co-operation	—	—	7	69	—	5
Religious and moral development of pupils	—	—	—	—	—	15
Not interested/ No expectations/ Little contact/ Do not know	—	4	1	6	4	17
Other	18	20	7	4	13	11
No reply	9	5	7	7	5	6
Total (%)	100	100	100	100	100	100

gramme. Almost equal percentages of men (38 per cent) and women teachers (40 per cent) felt this. Nineteen per cent of the respondents (23 per cent men, 18 per cent women) described

[11]Table 6.4 presents the analysis of replies to an open-ended question concerning what was perceived as *chiefly* expected of teachers by the counter positions. It may not be inferred from this table that when teachers stated that certain behaviour was *chiefly* expected of them by a counter position that they thought this was the *only* behaviour the incumbent of this position expected.

the inspector's main expectations as 'conscientious work'. Twelve per cent stated that the inspector demanded conformity to rules (15 per cent men, 11 per cent women). Some respondents (9 per cent) complained of the lack of understanding by the inspector.

(*iii*) *Principal:* Thirty-four per cent of the respondents said that the principal expected hard work, while a further 19 per cent said that adherence to the regulations was what the principal expected. There was little difference between the replies of men and women.

(*iv*) *Colleagues:* Almost 70 per cent of respondents felt that colleagues expected co-operation and loyalty. Of these only 8 per cent referred specifically to professional co-operation, such as sharing and discussing methods of teaching and seeking and giving advice on dealing with pupils. The rest referred to such qualities as friendliness and general helpfulness. This in itself is interesting as it may give a clue as to the kind of behaviour teachers consider gives status among colleagues. It is noteworthy that examination successes by pupils were not mentioned by any respondent. Again there was little difference between the responses of men and women.

(*v*) *Parents:* Both men and women teachers perceived parents as chiefly expecting them to teach the prescribed programme (51 per cent). However, more men (21 per cent) than women (9 per cent) felt that parents expected examination success, while women more frequently felt that parents demanded kindness and understanding (women 53 per cent, men 31 per cent).

(*vi*) *Manager:* A wide range of replies was received to the question on managers' expectations. Among men, the most numerous replies referred to the managers' concern with the religious and moral development of pupils (23 per cent), with maintaining the status quo (17 per cent) and with conscientious work (15 per cent). Women, however, most frequently said that they had no contact with the manager (23 per cent). Nineteen per cent of women respondents stated that the manager expected conscientious work, while 12 per cent stated that he expected the religious and moral development of pupils and a further 12 per cent said he expected the maintenance of the status quo.

From the above presentation it can be concluded that the incumbents of the various counter positions were seen by respondents to hold different expectations for teachers. While pupils were perceived as chiefly expecting kindness, understanding and good example from the teacher, the inspector and principal were thought to expect chiefly the teaching of the prescribed programme, conscientious work and conformity to rules. Colleagues were perceived as expecting loyalty and co-operation and parents as expecting the prescribed programme to be taught, and such qualities as kindness and understanding. The manager was seen as chiefly expecting conscientious work, the religious and moral development of pupils and the maintenance of the status quo.

It would appear that pupils and parents were seen as chiefly expecting rather similar behaviour from the teacher. The inspector, principal and manager were also thought to have rather similar expectations, tending to emphasize conscientious work and conformity to rules more frequently than did pupils and parents. Colleagues were felt to have a unique set of expectations, those of loyalty and co-operation.

There appeared to be more consensus among respondents concerning the chief expectations of pupils and colleagues than there was concerning the expectations of the other counter positions studied. Seventy-one per cent of the respondents agreed that pupils expected such things as kindness, and 69 per cent were agreed that colleagues expected co-operation.

3. *Summary of the Role-Set of Teachers.* It may be concluded from the above discussion, firstly, that only pupils were seen as having any great influence on the teacher's work; secondly, that a wide variation existed between the perceived expectations

of different counter positions; and thirdly, that there was some disagreement among respondents as to what the incumbents of each position chiefly expected. In general there was little difference between expectations as perceived by men and by women. However, one difference which did occur was that women more frequently than men felt that pupils expected such characteristics as kindness and understanding and thought that pupils had more influence on their work.

Summary of the Role of the Teacher

From the findings reported in this chapter it appears that Dublin national teachers see teaching as a wide-ranging activity, involving the attainment of such relatively diffuse goals as the moral, intellectual and social development of their pupils. It would seem that they feel that these goals are achieved in more ways than simply by teaching the prescribed programme which is felt to be less obligatory for teachers than the giving of good example. There is nothing very specialized about giving good example; it is a continuous activity and Dublin teachers feel that it is not confined to school hours but may go on after school hours too. In an industrializing society where the trend is towards impersonal relationships in work, the teacher's commitment to a personal relationship with his pupils may be difficult to accept and to maintain.

Respondents stated that pupils influenced their work more than any other position in their role-set. They felt that pupils most frequently expected kindness, understanding and to be given good example by the teacher. It could well be that teachers feel that fulfilment of these expectations may be the way to bring about their pupils' general development to which they feel so highly committed.

The investigation of the role-set of teachers proved valuable. The high influence of 'pupil' and the low influence of 'manager' are noteworthy. Indeed the relatively low ranking of all positions except 'pupil' indicates that teachers consider themselves relatively independent in their work. It might have been thought that the wide variety of positions related to teaching and the different expectations for the teacher held by the incumbents of these positions would cause many conflicts. However, irrespective of how many or how varied the positions involved in a role-set are they do not cause undue conflict for the incumbents of the focal position if they have little influence on them. The causes and implications of the teachers' independence are further discussed in the concluding chapter.

In general, men and women put similar emphasis on certain aspects of teaching, felt similar counter positions to be influential, and perceived similar expectations from the incumbents of different counter positions. There were some differences, however. Women, somewhat more frequently than men, tended to emphasize the importance of their pupils' influence on their work, to feel that pupils expected kindness and understanding, to feel obliged to give special help to backward children, to try to ensure that pupils grew up good Christians, and to teach the prescribed programme.

The role dimension of this study, then, appears to throw considerable light on the position of the national teacher in Dublin. It clarifies the aims of teachers and gives some insight into the relationships between teachers and others in related positions. In addition it appears to this writer that the role definition instrument used in this study could give some insight into the values of society, while recognizing that the two concepts—role definition and values—are analytically different. The score on each item of the instrument indicates in some way the importance attached by teachers to the values embodied in each of the items. Teachers, as a group, communicate the value system of a society. Accordingly, their scores on the role definition instrument may be some indication of the relative importance of certain values in Irish society. It would indeed be most interesting if one could obtain cross-cultural scores on this or a similar instrument, for this might well highlight differences between societies in their value systems.

CHAPTER VII

PARENT-TEACHER RELATIONS

THE analysis of the role-set of teachers was extended by examining more fully the relationship between teachers and parents. This relationship was intensively investigated because many studies have shown that the child's progress in school depends to an extraordinary degree on the educational quality of his home background, and on the stimulus and support his home gives him throughout his schooldays.[1]

The child is involved in two agencies of socialization, the home and the school. Ideally each should perform complementary educational functions. However, many factors may inhibit the achievement of this ideal, of which the most serious is lack of contact between teachers and parents, with the consequent absence of communication. This may be accentuated if different value orientations are held in the home and in the school.

There is a great necessity for communication between parents and teachers since it is to the advantage of both, but especially to the child. This contact fosters greater understanding by both parent and teacher of their respective aims and can promote a greater parental interest in the formal education of the child. This parental interest and encouragement of the child has, as

[1] In this connection see: H. Becker, 'The Teacher in the Authority System of the School', in A. Etzioni, *Complex Organizations*, New York, 1961, pp. 243-251; B. Bernstein, 'Social Structure, Language and Learning', *Educational Research*, Vol. III, No. 3, June 1961, pp. 163-176; J. Coleman et al., *Equality of Educational Opportunity*, Washington, US Department of Health, Education and Welfare, 1966; K. Cullen, *School and Family*, Dublin, 1969; J. W. B. Douglas, *The Home and the School*, London, 1964; J. E. Floud, A. H. Halsey and F. M. Martin, *Social Class and Educational Opportunity*, London, 1956; A. B. Holingshead, *Elmtown's Youth*, New York, 1949; S. Wiseman, *Education and Environment*, Manchester University Press 1964.

one writer points out, '. . . an important bearing upon school motivation and performance.'[2] Furthermore, to quote Dr Douglas:

> In each social class, children have a considerable advantage in the eight-year tests if their parents take an interest in school work, and an even greater advantage at eleven. The influence of the level of the parents' interest on test performance is greater than that of . . . size of family, standard of home, and academic record of the school . . . it becomes increasingly important as the child grows older.[3]

Although contact with all parents is important, contact with parents who hold different values to those of the school and teacher may be the most necessary. British sociologists have emphasized the necessity of communication between teachers and working-class parents. The values of the working class such as '. . . short-term goals and a . . . higher valuation on manual work than on book learning'[4] may be completely different from the values of the teacher. If the child from the working-class home is not to be pulled in two directions there must be contact and communication between home and school. Otherwise these differences in attitudes can lead to misunderstanding, non-co-operation and, in some cases, direct hostility.

Denis Marsden has described a group of working-class parents with children at grammar school who became involved in such difficulties because of the lack of communication between themselves and the school which their children attended.[5] He describes the experience of these parents as a feeling of a 'misunderstanding of needs . . . anxieties, the sense "of us" and "them", . . . social unease and . . . bewilderment . . .'[6]

[2]D. F. Swift, 'Social Class and Achievement Motivation', *Educational Research*, February 1966, cited in M. Craft et al. (Eds.) *Linking Home and School*, London, 1967, p. 190.

[3]J. W. B. Douglas, *The Home and the School*, London, 1964, p. 57.

[4]M. Craft, 'The Teacher/Social Worker', p. 189, in M. Craft et al., *op. cit.*, pp. 186-208.

[5]D. Marsden, 'Education and the Working Class', in M. Craft et al. (Eds.) *op. cit.*, pp. 48-61.

[6]*Ibid.*, p. 58.

Marsden has suggested that informal access to the teacher may be the best means of facilitating parent-teacher communication.[7] John Barron Mays, however, remarks that parent-teacher associations may be most fruitful.[8] He recognizes the possible hostility of teachers to these associations,[9] but believes that they are the means by which the tie between home and school can be made most stable.[10]

This study is a beginning in the direction of investigating the complex topic of parent-teacher relations in Ireland and more particularly in Dublin city. The survey concentrated on the attitudes of teachers[11] and studied three aspects of parent-teacher relations:

    I The form and extent of existing parent-teacher relations
   II The attitude of teachers to parents, and
  III The attitude of teachers to changes in parent-teacher relations.

Data on each of these topics will be related to the type of area from which the teachers' pupils came.

Form and Extent of Existing Parent-Teacher Relations
The existing pattern of parent-teacher relations is discussed under two headings:

  1. Degree and place of parent-teacher contact.
  2. The existence of formal parent-teacher associations or groups.

  1. *Degree and place of parent-teacher contact.* To investigate the degree and place of parent-teacher contact respondents were

[7] *Ibid.*, p. 60.
[8] J. B. Mays, 'The Impact of Neighbourhood Values', p. 77, in M. Craft et al. (Eds.) *op. cit.*, pp. 62-79.
[9] *Ibid.*, p. 72.
[10] *Ibid.*, p. 77.
[11] For a study of the attitudes of parents, see K. Cullen, *School and Family*, Dublin, 1969.

asked how much contact they had had with the parents of pupils since the beginning of the school year (1 July 1966). They were asked whether they had met:

1. Most of them
2. Some of them
3. Very few of them

either in school (question 12a) or outside school (question 12b).

The results obtained from an analysis of replies to these questions are given in Table 7·1. Concerning meetings with parents at the school, 17 per cent of the respondents had met most of the parents, 38 per cent had met some, while 39 per cent had met very few of them. Meetings with parents outside school were infrequent, one respondent had met most of the parents outside school, 8 per cent had met some, while 85 per cent had met very few. It can thus be seen that only a small minority (17 per cent) of the teachers had met most of the parents of their pupils. When meetings did occur, the place of contact between parents and teachers tended to be in the school rather than outside it.

TABLE 7·1

Meetings of Parents and Teachers by Place of Meeting

| Parents Visited the School | Parents met outside School | | | | | | | | |
| | Very few | | Some | | Most | | No reply | | Total | |
	N	%	N	%	N	%	N	%	N	%
Very few	56	37	3	2	—	—	—	—	59	39
Some	53	35	5	3	—	—	—	—	58	38
Most	19	13	5	3	1	1	—	—	25	17
No reply	—	—	—	—	—	—	9	6	9	6
Total	128	85	13	8	1	1	9	6	151	100

The relationship between the type of area in which the parents lived and the number of the parents who visited the school is set out in Table 7.2.

TABLE 7.2

Extent of Respondents' Contact at School with Parents, related to type of Area from which Pupils came

Type of Area	Extent of Contact (percentage)				Total (N)
	Most called %	Some called %	Very few called %	No reply %	
Poor City Centre Area	—	37	54	8	24
Corporation pre-1939 Estate	13	40	47	—	15
Corporation post-1944 Estate	12	37	43	8	60
Privately owned housing	29	41	25	4	51
Total	17	38	39	6	150

It may be noted from this table that teachers had least contact with parents from poor centre city areas and most contact with parents who lived in privately owned houses. None of the respondents teaching children from poor centre city areas had met most of their parents and over half of them (54 per cent) stated that very few of the parents visited the school. On the other hand, almost 30 per cent of the teachers of pupils from private houses had met most of the parents and only 25 per cent stated that they had met very few parents. However, the extent of the contact of teachers with parents in any area can hardly be regarded as great.

2. *The Existence of Parent-Teacher Associations or Groups.* Respondents were also asked to indicate whether a parent-teacher association or group of any kind existed in their school, and if so to give details of it (question 13). Twenty per cent of the respondents (10 per cent of men and 25 per cent of women) reported that there was some type of parent-teacher association or group in their school. Two kinds of meetings were most frequently mentioned: (a) Meetings to discuss some particular business as for example arrangements for First Communion or

Confirmation, to raise funds or to hear a talk by an expert (8 per cent), (b) Meetings held at the beginning or the end of each year for the expressed purpose of enabling teachers to meet parents (6 per cent).

When the existence of parent-teacher associations is related to the type of area from which pupils came (Table 7.3), the dearth of such associations in centre city areas can be noted. Ninety-six per cent of the teachers in these areas stated that there was no parent-teacher association or group in their school. The corresponding figure for Corporation pre-1939 estates is 93 per cent, while that for both Corporation post-1944 estates and areas of privately owned housing is 75 per cent.

TABLE 7.3

Existence of Parent-Teacher Associations or Groups, related to the type of Area from which Pupils came

Parent-Teacher Association	Type of Area (percentage)				Total
	Centre City	Pre-1939 Estate	Post-1944 Estate	Privately Owned	
	%	%	%	%	%
No Parent-Teacher Association	96	93	75	75	80
Parent-Teacher Association	4	7	25	25	20
Total (N)	24	15	60	51	

From the above discussion it may be concluded that there was not a great deal of contact between national teachers and parents of their pupils in Dublin city. When meetings did take place, they appeared most often to take the form of the parent calling to the school to meet the teacher. There was very little contact between parents and teachers outside the school and few schools had parent-teacher associations or groups of any kind. These trends were particularly marked in schools in poor city centre areas.

Attitude of Teachers to Parents
The attitude of respondents to parents is discussed under three headings:

1. Degree of satisfaction with the attitude of parents to education
2. Degree of satisfaction with parent-teacher relations
3. Extent to which parents were seen by respondents as preventing them from achieving their ideals.

1. *Degree of Satisfaction with the Attitude of Parents to Education.*
Respondents were asked to state their satisfaction or dissatisfaction with the attitude of parents to education. The results are presented in Table 7.4. It can be seen that 51 per cent of the respondents said they were either very satisfied or satisfied with parents' attitude to education. Men were more critical than women, 60 per cent of them stating that they were dissatisfied or very dissatisfied, compared to 43 per cent of women.

TABLE 7.4

Degree of Satisfaction with Attitude of Parents to Education

Degree of Satisfaction	Men		Women		Total	
	N	%	*N*	%	*N*	%
Very Satisfied	4	8	12	12	16	11
Satisfied	14	29	46	45	60	40
Dissatisfied	19	40	30	29	49	32
Very Dissatisfied	10	21	14	14	24	16
No reply	1	2	1	1	2	1
Total	48	100	103	100	151	100

Respondents teaching pupils from centre city areas were most dissatisfied with the attitude of parents to education, 50 per cent of them stating that they were very dissatisfied and 25 per cent that they were dissatisfied.[12] Likewise 27 per cent of teachers of

[12]See Table A.26, Appendix 1.

pupils from Corporation pre-1939 estates were very dissatisfied and 53 per cent dissatisfied. However, none of the teachers of pupils from privately owned housing stated that they were very dissatisfied, while 76 per cent said they were satisfied.

2. *Degree of Satisfaction with Parent-Teacher relations.* Respondents were asked to state their degree of satisfaction or dissatisfaction with relations with parents, and the results are given in Table 7.5. This table shows that 67 per cent of the respondents said they were satisfied with parent-teacher relations. Women were significantly more satisfied (72 per cent) than men (55 per cent). It is interesting that the female respondents who had no parent-teacher association in their school were more satisfied (76 per cent) with parent-teacher relations than were female respondents who had such an association (60 per cent, n=25).

TABLE 7.5

Degree of Satisfaction with Relations with Parents

Degree of Satisfaction	Men		Women		Total	
	N	%	N	%	N	%
Very Satisfied	8	17	26	25	34	23
Satisfied	18	38	48	47	66	44
Dissatisfied	17	35	23	22	40	27
Very Dissatisfied	5	10	4	4	9	6
No reply	—	—	2	2	2	1
Total	48	100	103	100	151	100

It is noteworthy that satisfaction with relations with parents is greater among respondents whose pupils came from privately owned housing (78 per cent) than among respondents whose pupils came from any other type of area.[13]

3. *Extent to which Parents were seen by Respondents as preventing them from achieving their ideals.* Respondents were asked by means of an open-ended question (Question 9a) if there were any

[13]See Table A.27., Appendix 1.

factors which prevented them from achieving their ideals as teachers. Eighty-three per cent of respondents mentioned some factors,[14] and twenty per cent stated that parents prevented them from achieving their ideals. Most of these respondents complained of the lack of interest and non co-operation of parents. Men (29 per cent) more frequently complained of parents than did women (16 per cent). When these results were cross-tabulated by pupils' area of residence it was again found that city centre teachers most frequently (41 per cent) said that they found parents a problem.[15] This was stated by 13 per cent of teachers in Corporation pre-1939 estates and 21 per cent of teachers in post-1944 estates. It was least frequently (9 per cent) mentioned by teachers of pupils from privately owned housing.

Some of the comments which teachers made when answering the above question are interesting. Of those who were dissatisfied with relations with parents these remarks are typical:

—Parents come from poorer centre city areas, and are not very much interested in education;
—They can't be otherwise than disinterested as conditions are in this district;
—Too many have either no interest or expect miracles;
—Parents do not understand teachers' difficulties;
—I find some aggressive (I think they must be anti-authority anyway); they don't seem to think that I might be doing my best for the children.

Of those who expressed satisfaction the following remarks were representative:

—The parents of the children in my class this year are very interested. They help the pupils at home (reading stories);
—They are almost all from the professional class and appreciate our efforts and respect us;
—Most of them are very interested and help when they can;
—Parents are very appreciative of teacher's interest in their children.

[14]See Table 8.5, p. 92.
[15]See Table A.28, Appendix 1.

In conclusion to this section it may be said that there appeared to be a strong relationship between the area from which parents came and the degree to which teachers' attitudes towards them were favourable. Teachers appeared to perceive parents from poor centre city areas as uninterested in education, unsatisfactory in their relationships with the teacher and as impediments to the achievement of their ideals. At the other extreme teachers appeared to see parents from private housing in a much more favourable light and as satisfactory in their attitude to education and relations with the teacher.

Attitude of Teachers to Changes in Parent-Teacher Relations

This section is divided into three parts:

1. Attitude of respondents to changes in parent-teacher relationships
2. Form of relations with parents favoured by respondents
3. Further comments by respondents on parent-teacher relations.

1. *Attitude of Respondents to Changes in Parent-Teacher Relationships.* Respondents were asked whether they would like to see some changes in parent-teacher relations and whether they felt parents would welcome similar changes (questions 14 and 15). Replies to both these questions were analysed and are set out in Table 7.6.

TABLE 7.6

Degree of Contact Respondents would like with Parents, and Degree of Contact they felt Parents would like with them

Degree of Contact	Men		Women		Total	
	Teachers %	Parents %	Teachers %	Parents %	Teachers %	Parents %
More than at present	60	27	46	28	50	28
No change	33	58	53	61	47	60
Less than at present	6	4	1	2	3	3
Don't know	—	2	—	8	—	6
Other	—	2	—	—	—	1
No reply	—	6	—	1	—	3
Total %	100	100	100	100	100	100
Total N	48	48	103	103	151	151

It can be seen from this table that respondents were more in favour of changes in parent-teacher relations than they thought parents were. Men were more inclined to feel this way than women.

Fifty per cent of the teachers stated that they wanted more contact with parents than at present but only 28 per cent felt that parents would welcome such a change. Indeed 60 per cent of them felt that parents would favour 'no change' from the present state of parent-teacher contact.

The replies of respondents concerning preferred changes in parent-teacher relations were cross-tabulated by their replies concerning what changes they thought parents would like.[16] It was found that of the 50 per cent of respondents who said they would like more contact with parents only half of these thought that parents would like more contact with them.

A considerably higher percentage of men (60 per cent) than women (46 per cent) wished for more contact with parents, while a significantly greater percentage of women (53 per cent) than men (33 per cent) wanted no change. It will be remembered that men were consistently more dissatisfied with parent-teacher relations and more critical of the attitude of parents to education than were women.

It is of interest to note that the amount of contact respondents had with parents was not related to the desire for more or less contact. The two categories of teachers—those who wanted more contact and those who did not—had a similar amount of contact with parents. Likewise, there was no significant difference between the same two categories when compared with the proportion who had parent-teacher associations in their schools. Of the 30 respondents who said there was a parent-teacher association in their school 50 per cent said they wished for more contact with parents, which is the same as the corresponding figure for all respondents.

The relationship between the changes teachers favoured and what they thought parents favoured was examined in terms of the area from which pupils came.[17] The greatest discrepancy

[16]See Tables A.29 and A.30, Appendix 1.
[17]See Tables A.25 and A.31, Appendix 1.

between the changes favoured by teachers and those which they felt parents favoured was found in the poor city centre area. While 63 per cent of the teachers in this area said they would like more contact, only 13 per cent of them felt that parents were of the same opinion. Rather, 75 per cent of them felt that parents would prefer no change. The least discrepancy was found for teachers of pupils from privately owned housing; 37 per cent of these stated they would like more contact, and 33 per cent said that parents would like more.

It is of interest to note that while the discrepancy between teachers' preferences and the supposed preferences of parents was greatest in the poorer areas, the teachers in these areas were those who most frequently stated that they wanted more contact with the parents of their pupils. Sixty-three per cent of teachers in poor city centre areas, and 53 per cent and 57 per cent in Corporation pre-1939 and post-1944 estates respectively, wanted more contact with parents. Only 37 per cent of teachers of pupils from privately owned housing wanted this change.

To sum up, it would appear that half of the respondents wanted more contact with parents; half of these, however, felt that parents did not want more contact with them. This trend was particularly marked in city centre areas. Also, a higher proportion of men than women wanted more contact with parents.

2. *Form of Relations with Parents favoured by Respondents.* As part of the intensive examination of relationships between parents and teachers, respondents were asked what form of parent-teacher relations they preferred. Six possible forms of parent-teacher relationships were presented to the respondents (question 16), who were asked to rank them (1–6) according to their preferences. The six possibilities, formulated after preliminary discussions with teachers, were:

1. Formal parent-teacher associations
2. Period of ordinary school time to be allotted to meeting parents
3. No special arrangements, but that the teacher sees parents if they call to the school

4. Teachers to be available in the school one evening a month to meet parents
5. A special meeting be called in the school once or twice a year at which teacher, manager and parents are present
6. No opportunity be given to parents of meeting the teacher

A summary of the results is presented here.[18] A rank score was obtained for each form of parent-teacher relations by multiplying the number of respondents in each particular rank by the appropriate numerical weighting (1–6) of the rank, adding together the products, and dividing the result by the total number who responded. The procedure may be seen more clearly from the following example, in which a rank score for 'formal parent-teacher associations' was calculated.

Formal Parent-Teacher Associations

	Rank 1	Rank 2	Rank 3	Rank 4	Rank 5	Rank 6	Total
Number replying	7	8	19	30	58	7	129
Weighted Rank	7×1	8×2	19×3	30×4	58×5	7×6	
	7 +	16 +	57 +	120 +	290 +	42	$=532$

$$\frac{532}{129} = 4 \cdot 1$$

Rank Score $= 4 \cdot 1$

Rank scores were thus calculated for each form of parent-teacher relationships. These scores are given in Table 7.7.

[18]Results were analysed by counting the number and calculating the percentage of respondents who put each given form of parent-teacher relations in the various ranks (1-6). Tables were constructed giving this information for each form of parent-teacher relations. These detailed tables are given in Appendix 1, Tables A.33 to A.38. The high proportion of non-response to some items is due to the fact that some respondents marked only their first choice.

TABLE 7.7

Rank score and rank position of each form of Parent-Teacher relations

Form of Parent-Teacher Relations	Rank Score	Rank Position
No special arrangements but teacher sees parents if they call to the school	2·0	1
Period of ordinary school time to be allotted to meeting parents	2·6	2
A special meeting be called in the school once or twice a year at which teacher, manager and parents are present	3·0	3
Teachers to be available in the school one evening a month to meet parents	3·1	4
Formal Parent-Teacher Associations	4·1	5
No opportunity be given to parents of meet- the teacher	5·7	6

It can be seen from this table that teachers preferred informal to formal parent-teacher relations, while 'no opportunity be given to parents of meeting the teacher' was ranked last. The form of parent-teacher relations most favoured by respondents was 'no special arrangements but teacher sees parents if they call to the school'. Fifty per cent of all respondents ranked this form number 1 (Table 7.8).[19]

The small proportion who preferred formal parent-teacher associations (5 per cent) is noteworthy. Teachers in poor centre city areas appeared rather less favourable to parent-teacher associations than did teachers from other areas.[20]

The dislike of parent-teacher associations was also in evidence in replies to the question which asked whether or not respondents felt obliged as teachers to arrange such meetings.[21] Twenty-three per cent of the respondents stated that teachers

[19]Note that in Table 7.8 first choices only are presented while in calculating rank scores (Table 7.7) the number allotting each numerical weighting (1-6) was considered.
[20]See Table A.32, Appendix 1.
[21]See Chapter VI above, also Table A.7, Appendix 1.

TABLE 7.8

Number and percentage of respondents who ranked the given forms of Parent-Teacher relations first

Forms of Parent-Teacher Relations	Men		Women		Total	
	N	%	N	%	N	%
No special arrangements but teacher sees parents if they call to the school	22	46	54	52	76	50
Period of ordinary school time to be allotted to meeting parents	7	15	22	21	29	19
A special meeting be called in the school once or twice a year at which teacher, manager and parents are present	11	23	11	11	22	15
Teachers to be available in the school one evening a month to meet parents	5	10	10	10	15	10
Formal Parent-Teacher associations	2	4	5	5	7	5
No opportunity be given to parents of meeting the teacher	1	2	—	—	1	1
Total	48	100	102	100	150	100

'absolutely should not' arrange parent-teacher meetings, 20 per cent stated that teachers 'preferably should not' and 30 per cent said that teachers 'may or may not' arrange these meetings. However, higher proportions of respondents felt that teachers should ('absolutely must' and 'preferably should') send reports on pupils' progress to parents (72 per cent),[22] and invite parents of difficult pupils to come to see the teacher (91 per cent).[23]

[22]See Table A.3, Appendix 1.
[23]See Table A.5. Appendix 1.

D

3. *Further Comments of Teachers on Parent-Teacher Relations.*
Teachers were asked if they had any further comments on
parent-teacher relations. Half the respondents made some comments. Some of these are presented here to illustrate in more
detail teachers' attitudes to parents. While these comments
were chosen as representative, they cannot, strictly speaking,
be generalized to the whole survey population.

Three types of attitudes were prevalent in these comments.
The first acknowledged the importance of parent-teacher relations, the second stated a preference for informal rather than
formal parent-teacher relations and the third was critical of
parents.

In the first type of comment respondents stated that teachers
and parents should meet and co-operate for the good of the
child, as the following examples show:

—I think parents and teachers should collaborate closely in
educational matters—improved relations between them
would improve matters in the classroom—interest in
curriculum and progress of children could be beneficial to
teacher and children (female teacher, aged 51–60, working
with pupils from Corporation pre-1939 housing estate);

—The teacher who knows a child's parents, the type they
are and the home background, understands the child
better and is given an insight into the child's character.
This influences the teacher-child relations, usually to the
advantage of the child (female teacher, aged over 60,
working with pupils from privately owned houses);

—For some years past, I have sent for and met all the parents
individually—usually about 6 a week. I have found out
quite an amount about various children and have noticed,
quite often, a greater interest and understanding of what is
done in school. I have also found out several things, which
I am almost certain I would not have found out at a formal
meeting of parents (male teacher, aged under 30, working
with pupils from Corporation post-1944 housing estate);

—A certain amount of contact is necessary between parents and teachers. Environment plays a very important part in the upbringing of a child, and it is the teacher's obligation to get acquainted with his background. Many a child's education is impeded by conditions in the home, e.g. tension, disharmony between father and mother, poverty (female teacher, aged under 30, working with pupils from privately owned houses).

In the second type of comment teachers expressed a preference for informal non-compulsory meetings with parents in which a personal relationship could be fostered in a private and confidential setting. These teachers appeared to expect parents to initiate such meetings, and they stated that they would only get in touch with parents when a specific difficulty arose with regard to an individual pupil. The teachers who made such comments also disliked formal parent-teacher associations since they did not consider them conducive to private discussions with parents on the difficulties of each pupil. They also feared that these associations might be controlled by a vocal minority of parents to the exclusion of others, and that they might be used to criticize or dictate to the teacher. The following are examples of these comments:

—I am against parent-teacher associations. If a parent wishes to see the teacher for any particular reason concerning the child, or vice versa, let this be done when the parent brings or collects the child from school—this provides ample opportunity, and without compulsion of any sort in either case, (female teacher, aged under 30, working with pupils from poor city centre area);

—I think an informal parent-teacher relationship is the most suitable both for parents and teachers. The formal parent-teacher association tends to interfere too much with the freedom of the teacher and, besides, a certain vocal minority will control these meetings to the almost complete exclusion of the other parents (male teacher, aged under 30, working with pupils from privately owned houses);

—As the pupil-teacher relationship is personal I feel that the parent-teacher relationship should also be personal. Problems are usually individual ones and not for open discussion at a formal meeting, (female teacher, aged 41–50, working with pupils from Corporation pre-1939 housing estate);

—If I wish to see a parent I send a message to her and she comes during school hours and we discuss the child. If a parent has a problem she does likewise. I fail to see the purpose of the formal parent-teacher association because I would not like to discuss any child in the presence of a crowd. If parents have problems about the curriculum, we as teachers can make no change (female teacher, aged 41–50, working with pupils from privately owned houses);

—In Ireland parent-teacher associations are not advisable. Some busy-body would or might upset the apple cart (male teacher, aged 51–60, working with pupils from Corporation pre-1939 housing estate).

The third type of comment was critical of parents. Some criticisms appeared to be based on class prejudice and showed quite a degree of hostility.

Some examples of these comments are:

—I should not like parent-teacher associations in the area in which I teach. Most fathers are in Trade Unions and I fear parent-teacher associations might develop into trade union meetings, from which the Lord preserve us! (female teacher, aged 51–60, working with pupils from Corporation pre-1939 housing estate);

—I don't think parent-teacher associations would work in this district. Members of associations meet on a basis of equality (i.e. intellectually). Judging by the written communications I receive from parents I should say that most are practically illiterate. In my opinion, it would not be easy to 'reach' such parents and all discussion would be futile (male teacher, aged over 60, working with pupils from poor city centre area).

Conclusions and Implications

At the beginning of this chapter it was suggested that two of the more important factors which might limit parent-teacher co-operation were lack of contact between home and school and the different values held in each. It would appear from this study that both these factors limited communication between Dublin city teachers and the parents of their pupils.

The overall impression one receives from the investigation is that teachers work in relative isolation from parents. Only 17 per cent of the teachers stated that they had met most of their pupils' parents. The existing pattern of meeting parents and that desired for the future was of informal contact at the school. Only 20 per cent of the teachers stated that there was a parent-teacher association or group at their school, while only 5 per cent said that this was the form of parent-teacher relations they would favour most. Some teachers appeared to feel that informal contact rather than formal parent-teacher associations was more conducive to confidential discussions with parents since at these informal meetings the individual problems of pupils could be discussed in a personal way. They criticized formal parent-teacher associations because of the difficulty of personal contact with parents within them, and because they might be used against the teacher.[24]

Half the teachers were in favour of increased contact with parents, despite the fact that half of these felt that the parents involved would not desire this. Whether this impression was mistaken is not known and should be further investigated.

[24]Howard Becker, having interviewed sixty teachers in Chicago public schools, suggested that these teachers feared the intrusion of parents, even on legitimate grounds, because they felt that it would damage the authority of the teacher and make him subject to control by outsiders. See H. S. Becker, 'The Teacher in the Authority System of the School', in A. Etzioni, *Complex Organizations*, New York 1961, pp. 243-251.

These findings have two important implications for those who wish to increase contact between parents and teachers. Firstly, it indicates that if teachers are opposed to parent-teacher associations this does not mean that they are opposed to all forms of parent-teacher contact. Secondly, as many teachers appear to be opposed to parent-teacher associations it might be detrimental to parent-teacher relations to impose such groups on them without their consent. It might perhaps be better to begin by increasing the amount of informal contact between parents and teachers.

Parent-teacher relations in poor centre city areas appeared to cause greatest problems for teachers. City centre teachers were most critical of parents, had least contact with them and most frequently felt that parents would not like more contact with teachers.

It will be remembered that respondents most frequently came from farming or middle-class homes outside Dublin. The value orientations of these homes may be exemplified by these teachers' high regard for education and the postponement of immediate gratification for the sake of achieving a long term goal. In the system through which these teachers were educated competition was institutionalized and achievement rewarded. These values may be contrary to those held by the majority of working-class parents, and when this difference in value orientations exists between teachers and parents communication and co-operation become even more important. John Mays has suggested that '. . . the academic achievement (of children in socially deteriorated districts) will . . . improve only when teacher and parent work in close harmony with each other towards the attainment of commonly understood and agreed objectives.'[25]

Dublin teachers in centre city areas appeared to recognize this need for communication. A higher proportion of them (63 per cent) than of teachers in any other area said they wanted more contact with the parents of their pupils. However, while teachers seem to be aware of the necessity for increased contact

[25]J. B. Mays, *op. cit.*, p. 72.

they may not always fully understand the value orientations of these poor city centre areas.

Two practical suggestions may therefore be made in regard to these findings. The first is that it would appear to be a matter of considerable urgency that plans be developed for the improvement of parent-teacher relations in poorer areas. The second suggestion is that the teacher in these areas '. . . should have an awareness of the sub-cultures within our society and an awareness, particularly, of his own attitudes and assumptions towards them, in order to maximize the resources of each individual child regardless of social class.'[26]

---

[26]M. Craft, *op. cit.*, p. 189.

CHAPTER VIII

SATISFACTIONS AND DISSATISFACTIONS
OF TEACHERS

In this chapter four aspects of the job satisfaction of teachers will be discussed. These are:

    I The level of satisfaction of respondents with their work,
    II The factors which respondents said prevented them from achieving their ideals as teachers,
    III The sources of satisfaction and dissatisfaction of teachers, and
    IV Reasons for satisfaction and dissatisfaction with various aspects of teaching.

The findings of this study in relation to these four aspects will be presented and an attempt will be made to compare them to the findings of British and American studies on the job satisfaction of teachers.[1]

Level of Satisfaction of Teachers
Three approaches were used to study the level of satisfaction with teaching. These were:

    1. Degree of satisfaction of respondents with their work,
    2. Whether teaching as a career had lived up to the expectations respondents had for it before becoming teachers, and
    3. The advice respondents would give their son or daughter if he or she wished to become a teacher.

[1]See Chapter II, pp. 13-17.

1. *Degree of Satisfaction with Teaching.* In question 4 respondents were asked how satisfying they found their work as teachers. Four precoded response categories were used:[2]

1. Fully satisfying
2. Satisfying on the whole but not fully so
3. Moderately satisfying
4. Most unsatisfying.

The results are given in Table 8·1. It can be seen from this table that the general level of satisfaction appears to be quite high, only 2 per cent describing teaching as most unsatisfying.

TABLE 8.1

Level of satisfaction of respondents with their work as teachers

Level of Satisfaction	Men		Women		Total	
	N	%	N	%	N	%
Fully satisfying	8	17	38	37	46	31
Satisfying on the whole but not fully so	27	56	49	48	76	50
Moderately satisfying	9	19	15	15	24	16
Most unsatisfying	2	4	1	1	3	2
No reply	2	4	—	—	2	1
Total	48	100	103	100	151	100

Thirty-one per cent stated that they found teaching fully satisfying, 50 per cent stated that they found it satisfying on the whole but not fully so, while 16 per cent stated that they found it moderately satisfying. It is noteworthy that a significantly higher percentage of women (37 per cent) than men (17 per cent) said that they were fully satisfied with teaching. Women between the ages of 51 and 60 most frequently (50 per cent) stated that they were fully satisfied.[3] In the preliminary

[2] A similar question was asked by Rudd and Wiseman. But one difference between the question asked here and that of Rudd and Wiseman is that the precoded response category 'some satisfaction but not a great deal' used by Rudd and Wiseman was omitted. See W. G. A. Rudd and S. Wiseman, 'Sources of Dissatisfaction among a Group of Teachers', *cit. sup.*

[3] See Table A.39, Appendix 1.

investigations to this survey many teachers had commented on the high degree of frustration and low degree of satisfaction from teaching in city centre schools. However, when degree of satisfaction is cross-tabulated with the type of area from which respondents' pupils came, it can be seen (Table 8.2) that a relatively high proportion (58 per cent) of respondents with pupils from poor city centre areas said they were fully satisfied with teaching. It should also be noted that a higher proportion of respondents in this category said they found teaching 'moderately satisfying', while a smaller proportion said they found it 'satisfying on the whole but not fully so'. This suggests that teachers in poor city centre areas tended to be either highly satisfied or dissatisfied, with relatively few in between. A majority of teachers in all other types of area were in the 'in between' category, i.e. in the category 'satisfying on the whole but not fully so'.

TABLE 8.2

Level of satisfaction related to type of area from which pupils of respondents came

| Type of area | Level of satisfaction (percentage) | | | | |
	Fully satisfying	Satisfying on the whole	Moderately satisfying	Most unsatisfying	Total (N)
Poor City Centre Area	58	17	25	—	24
Corporation pre-1939 Estate	13	67	13	7	15
Corporation post-1944 Estate	27	55	13	2	60
Privately owned housing	27	55	15	2	51
Total	31	50	16	2	150

In an attempt to understand this result the replies of respondents from city centre schools were examined to see if there were any special factors which might account for the unexpected results in Table 8.2. It was concluded that the representation of various age and sex categories in the city centre sample did not account for its high proportion of 'fully satisfied'.[4]

Howard Becker found that in Chicago there was a tendency for teachers in city centre areas who were unhappy in their work to move to the suburbs. Some other teachers who adjusted to teaching in the city centre remained there.[5] It may be that the findings of the Dublin study reflect a similar pattern. It is noteworthy that 70 per cent of the city centre teachers were over 40 years of age compared to 49 per cent of the total sample. It may be that only those teachers who have adjusted to city centre teaching remain there. As the population in city centre areas is decreasing, relatively few new teachers are employed there, which might account for the high proportion of teachers over 40 years in these areas and for the fact that they are satisfied with their work.

2. *Whether teaching as a career had lived up to expectations.* Respondents were asked whether teaching as a career had lived up to the expectations they had for it before they became teachers (question 6). Four pre-coded response categories were used:

1. Definitely yes
2. In general, yes
3. In general, no
4. Definitely no

Answers to this question are analysed in Table 8.3. It can be seen from this table that 86 per cent of the respondents gave a positive reply to this question, either 'definitely yes' (20 per cent) or 'in general, yes' (66 per cent).

It may also be noted that a significantly higher percentage of women (26 per cent) than men (6 per cent) said teaching had

[4]See Table A.40, Appendix 1. It can be seen from this table that men and women under 40 years of age were under-represented in the city centre schools as compared with the city as a whole. While men under 40 years of age tended to be a dissatisfied group, women under 40 tended to be a satisfied group. Thus any differences that might have been caused by their under-representation in the city-centre schools were felt to be cancelled out.

[5]See: H. S. Becker, 'The career of the Chicago Public Schoolteacher,' *American Journal of Sociology*, Vol. 57, 1952, pp. 470-477.

definitely lived up to their expectations. This result is consistent with Table 8.1, page 87, which showed that a greater proportion of women than men said teaching was fully satisfying.

TABLE 8.3

Respondents' Opinions as to whether Teaching had lived up to their Expectations

Opinion	Men		Women		Total	
	N	%	N	%	N	%
Definitely yes	3	6	27	26	30	20
In general yes	35	73	65	63	100	66
In general no	8	17	10	10	18	12
Definitely no	1	2	1	1	2	1
No reply	1	2	—	—	1	1
Total	48	100	103	100	151	100

3. *Respondents' advice to their children on teaching.* A further attempt to gauge level of satisfaction with teaching was attempted by asking respondents what advice they would give their daughter (question 10) or son (question 11) if she or he were interested in becoming a national teacher and had the opportunity and ability to do so. These questions asked if the respondent's advice would be :

1. Definitely yes
2. Probably yes
3. Probably no
4. Definitely no.

The analysis of answers to these questions is presented in Table 8.4. This table shows that 40 per cent of the men respondents said they would 'definitely' or 'probably' advise their son to become a national teacher, while 78 per cent of them said they would advise their daughter to do so. Of the women respondents, 52 per cent said they would advise their son to

TABLE 8.4

Advice Respondents would give to their Sons and Daughters if they wished to become National Teachers

| | Men | | Women | | Total | |
Advice	Sons %	Daughters %	Sons %	Daughters %	Sons %	Daughters %
Definitely yes	13	38	22	42	19	40
Probably yes	27	40	30	42	29	41
Probably no	35	15	20	10	25	11
Definitely no	21	4	26	7	25	6
Other	2	2	—	—	1	1
No reply	2	2	1	—	1	1
Total	100	100	100	100	100	100
N=	48	48	103	103	151	151

become a teacher, while 84 per cent said they would advise their daughter to do so. It might be interpreted from this result that, by and large, most respondents saw national teaching as a good job for women but not necessarily as a good job for men. It is of interest that over half (56 per cent) the male teachers said that they would either probably or definitely advise their interested son not to follow their own footsteps. This point is further discussed in the concluding chapter.

From the evidence on level of satisfaction presented so far it would appear that men were not as satisfied as women. National teaching was frequently seen as a more desirable occupation for women than for men. Overall, about 18 to 20 per cent of the men and 12 to 14 per cent of the women were dissatisfied with teaching, a figure which is somewhat higher than might be expected on the basis of studies in the United States and Britain.[6]

[6]See Chapter II, pp. 13-16. W. G. A. Rudd and S. Wiseman, in their study discussed on p. 14 above, found that 8 per cent of the teachers they interviewed were dissatisfied with teaching. F. Herzberg et. al., in a review of the literature on the prevalence of job dissatisfaction among all types of workers, came to the following conclusion: 'In summary, an examination of more than 50 studies reported in the literature indicates that a minimum of 13 per cent of our working population expresses a generalized negative attitude to their job.' F. Herzberg et al., *Job Attitudes: Review of Research and Opinion*, Pittsburg, Psychological Service, 1957, p. 6.

Factors preventing teachers from achieving their ideals.

An open-ended question was included inviting respondents to name any factors which prevented them from achieving their ideals as teachers (question 9).

Six general categories of complaints were found in the replies: size of class, lack of teaching aids, parents, pupils, curriculum, and management and administration of the school. The analysis of replies in terms of these categories is presented in Table 8.5.

TABLE 8.5

Percentage of Respondents who said that each of the following factors prevented them from Achieving their Ideals*

Factor	Men %	Women %	Total %
Size of class	42	35	37
Lack of teaching aids	46	28	34
Parents	29	16	20
Pupils	23	19	20
Curriculum	27	14	18
Management and Administration of school	19	10	13
Others	31	13	19
None	6	22	17
No reply	6	—	2
Total (N)	48	103	151

*Some respondents mentioned more than one factor.

Teachers most frequently (37 per cent) perceived size of class as a factor which prevented them from achieving their ideals.[7] This factor was followed by lack of teaching aids (34 per cent); parents and pupils (each 20 per cent); curriculum (18 per cent) and management and administration of school (13 per cent).

When respondents complained of class size, they all stated that

[7] For details on this and following complaints see Tables A.49 to A.55, Appendix I.

the classes which were too large inhibited good teaching or giving individual attention to pupils. Concerning teaching aids they complained of the lack of equipment, library or facilities for hobbies. In criticising the curriculum, they complained that it was too narrow and that too much time was spent on Irish. For a further discussion of these complaints see section IV of this chapter.

The teachers who stated that pupils were a factor limiting the achievement of their ideals tended to comment on the differential abilities of pupils in their class, their low intelligence, and on diversions outside school which distracted pupils' attention. When parents were mentioned teachers commented on their lack of interest and non-co-operation. On management and administration teachers complained of poor school buildings, the lack of heating, poor cleaning facilities and sometimes of the attitude of the principal and inspector.

The 'other' category included complaints about inadequate training, low salary and feelings of personal inadequacy.

It can also be seen from Table 8.5 that a higher percentage of men than women consistently mentioned each of the factors as inhibiting them from achieving their ideals. For men, lack of teaching aids (46 per cent), followed by size of class (42 per cent) were seen as the chief factors militating against them. For women size of class (35 per cent) was the main complaint, followed by lack of teaching aids (28 per cent). Twenty-two per cent of the women stated that there were no factors inhibiting the achievement of their ideals, while only 6 per cent of the men said this. This is in keeping with the general finding reported in this chapter that women were more satisfied with teaching than men. Women between the ages of 51 and 60 most frequently had no complaints (35 per cent), while all men over 30 years old said that there were some factors which prevented them from achieving their ideals.[8]

Sources of satisfaction and dissatisfaction in Teaching
It was felt that the best way of locating sources of satisfaction and dissatisfaction in teaching was to present a check-list of

[8]See Table A.56, Appendix 1.

possible sources and ask respondents to rate their degree of
satisfaction or dissatisfaction with each of the items on it. This
list was developed from preliminary discussions with teachers
and was pre-tested in the pilot survey. In responding to each of
the items on the check-list (question 18a) respondents were
given a choice of four answers:

1. Very satisfied
2. Satisfied
3. Unsatisfied
4. Very unsatisfied.

In the analysis of replies the number in each response category
(from 'very satisfied' to 'very unsatisfied') was counted. On this
basis, tables were prepared for each item showing the percentage of men, women, and the total percentage giving a particular response to each item. These tables are given in Appendix 1.[9] A summary of results obtained by calculating a satisfaction-dissatisfaction score (the mean, $\bar{X}$) for each item is
given in Table 8.6. The variance (V) was calculated separately
for each item as a measure of consensus among respondents on
replies to each item.[10] Differences between the scores and
differences between the variances for men and women were
tested for significance at the 5 per cent level.

It can be seen from Table 8.6 that provision of teaching aids
($\bar{X}=3.6$) and size of class ($\bar{X}=3.2$) were the two aspects of
teaching with which respondents were most dissatisfied. This
supports the finding reported in Table 8.5 that size of class and
lack of teaching aids were the chief factors preventing teachers
from achieving their ideals. The similarity of these two results,
obtained from different types of questions, would suggest
strongly that these are the two most common sources of teachers'
dissatisfaction in their work.

Other factors with which teachers were dissatisfied were the
opportunities for promotion ($\bar{X}=3.0$), teacher training
($\bar{X}=3.0$), the curriculum ($\bar{X}=2.8$) and salary ($\bar{X}=2.5$).

[9]Tables A.57 to A.74.
[10]The mean ($\bar{X}$) and variance (V) for each item was calculated by using a
method similar to that used in Chapter VI on the RDI, pp. 47-8.

TABLE 8.6

Satisfaction-Dissatisfaction Scores (X̄) and Variance (V) of Respondents on each item of the Satisfaction-Dissatisfaction Check-list

		Men	Women	Sig. Diff.	Total	Rank Order
Relations with colleagues	X̄	1·3	1·3	—	1·3	1
	V	0·2	0·3	—	0·3	
Holidays	X̄	1·5	1·6	—	1·5	2
	V	0·5	0·4	—	0·4	
Working with children	X̄	1·6	1·5	· · ·	1·5	2
	V	0·4	0·4	—	0·4	
Relations with principal	X̄	1·5	1·5	—	1·5	2
	V	0·5	0·5	—	0·5	
Relations with manager	X̄	1·8	1·6	—	1·7	5
	V	0·7	0·6	—	0·6	
Discipline in school	X̄	1·8	1·7	—	1·8	6
	V	0·5	0·5	—	0·5	
Hours of work	X̄	1·7	1·8	—	1·8	6
	V	0·4	0·4	—	0·4	
Relations with inspectors	X̄	1·9	1·9	—	1·9	8
	V	0·8	0·7	—	0·7	
Relations with parents	X̄	2·4	2·0	Sig.	2·2	9
	V	0·7	0·6	—	0·7	
Attitude of pupils to education	X̄	2·5	2·2	Sig.	2·3	10
	V	0·5	0·6		0·5	
Respect and recognition from public	X̄	2·7	2·3	Sig.	2·4	11
	V	0·8	0·7	—	0·7	
Attitude of parents to education	X̄	2·7	2·4	—	2·5	12
	V	0·8	0·8	—	0·8	
Salary	X̄	3·1	2·2	Sig.	2·5	12
	V	0·6	0·4	Sig.	0·7	
Curriculum	X̄	3·1	2·5	Sig.	2·8	14
	V	0·5	0·7	Sig.	0·6	
Training for teaching	X̄	2·9	3·1	—	3·0	15
	V	0·7	0·8	—	0·7	
Opportunities for promotion	X̄	3·3	2·9	Sig.	3·0	15
	V	0·7	0·7	—	0·7	
Size of Class	X̄	3·1	3·2	—	3·2	17
	V	0·8	0·8	—	0·8	
Provision of teaching aids	X̄	3·6	3·5	—	3·6	18
	V	0·5	0·5	—	0·5	

About mid-point between satisfied and dissatisfied were 'relations with parents' ($\bar{X}=2\cdot2$), 'attitude of parents to education' ($\bar{X}=2\cdot5$), and 'attitude of pupils to education' ($\bar{X}=2\cdot3$).

At the 'satisfied' end of the scale, it may be seen that relations with colleagues ($\bar{X}=1\cdot3$) is the aspect of teaching with which respondents said they were most satisfied. This is followed by 'holidays' ($\bar{X}=1\cdot5$), 'working with children' ($\bar{X}=1\cdot5$) and 'relations with principal' ($\bar{X}=1\cdot5$).

Relations with manager has a score of $1\cdot7$ which shows considerable satisfaction. It would appear then that while teachers have very little contact with the manager (cf. Chapter VI, page 57 ff.) they are not dissatisfied with this. 'Discipline in school' and 'hours of work' both have scores of $1\cdot8$ while 'relations with inspector' scores $1\cdot9$, which is indicative of considerable satisfaction with these aspects of teaching.

Significant differences in satisfaction-dissatisfaction scores between men and women were recorded on six items and it is interesting that on all of these men were less satisfied than women. These items are 'relations with parents', 'attitude of pupils to education', 'respect and recognition from the public', 'salary', 'curriculum' and 'opportunities for promotion'. Three of these items ('respect and recognition from the public', 'salary' and 'opportunities for promotion') are concerned with rewards from teaching in terms of remuneration and prestige.

It can be concluded from the above presentation that the main satisfactions for teachers were centred around 'relations with colleagues' and 'working with children'. The main dissatisfactions were the 'provision of teaching aids' and 'size of class'. Men also appeared particularly dissatisfied with 'opportunities for promotion' and 'salary'. In the following section the reasons given by respondents for being satisfied or dissatisfied with each of these items are discussed.

Reasons for satisfaction or dissatisfaction with various aspects of teaching

In addition to rating their degree of satisfaction or dissatisfaction with each item on the check-list, respondents were also asked to give brief reasons for their answers (question 18b). In analysing their replies considerable difficulty was encountered in developing response categories. Accordingly, it was decided that rather than undertaking an extensive statistical analysis it would be more useful to present examples of the actual answers given to each item with an indication of the frequency with which an answer of that type occurred. Each item is presented separately in the order in which it appears in Table 8.6, page 95.[11] Thus, the sources of satisfaction come first.

(i) *Relations with Colleagues.* Score 1·3.[12] This is the item with which respondents were most satisfied, ninety-seven per cent of them stating that they were 'very satisfied', or 'satisfied'. Typical comments were:
—All very helpful and interesting;
—We are a happy family, thank God;
—Dedicated staff;
—A good spirit prevails.
The only unfavourable comments were those of a few teachers who said they had little contact with the rest of the staff or did not meet them outside school.

(ii) *Holidays.* Score 1·5. This was one of the items with which most satisfaction was expressed. Ninety-three per cent of respondents said they were satisfied with it. Several of them, however, pointed out the need for long holidays in a job like teaching, and others suggested a mid-term break at the end of October.

(iii) *Working with Children.* Score 1·5. Ninety-three per cent of respondents said they were satisfied with this aspect of teaching. Replies such as the following were typical:
—I adore working with children and helping them, especially infants; I am only sorry that I cannot give them more individual attention;

[11]For further details on each item see Tables A.57 to A.74, Appendix 1.
[12]After each item, the satisfaction-dissatisfaction score on that item is given (as in Table 8.6). These scores must range between 1·0 (very satisfied) and 4·0 (very dissatisfied).

—Young children especially are so much themselves, so straight-forward and yet real people;
—I feel I can do far more for them than for adults;
—I like children;
—I find them well-mannered and responsive;
—I find working with children challenging, interesting and rewarding.

Among the few complaints were the following:
—Children are cross-eyed from T.V. No co-operation from parents;
—Numbers are sometimes frustrating;
—Tend to wear one out. Holidays are not long enough in which to recover.

(iv) *Relations with Principal.* Score 1·5. Ninety per cent of respondents said they were satisfied with relations with the principal of their school. The following replies are representative:
—He is 100% human and 'pulls' instead of throwing his weight;
—He consults staff on school matters. Periodic meetings;
—He is most considerate and helpful;
—She is very competent, fair and good humoured. Works very hard.

The following replies are illustrative of those who complained:
—The lay staff are not consulted as much as informed;
—Principals (nuns) change too often.

(v) *Relations with Manager.* Score 1·7. Eighty-five per cent of respondents said they were satisfied with relations with the school manager. The reason most commonly given was that the manager did not interfere in the work of the school:
—He expects us to do our work and keeps out of our way, so that we may do so;
—It's fairly satisfactory to have a manager who does not interfere;

—He never interferes when he knows that the teacher is doing his job well;

—Out of sight, out of mind.

The following replies are indicative of those who were not satisfied with relations with the manager:

—He is very friendly and helpful but has too many other duties and not enough money for the school;

—The only time we asked to meet him he refused;

—The manager is a grumpy, sometimes unreasonable old man with little interest in the school;

—He has too much authority, and generally little interest in the school.

(vi) *Discipline in School.* Score 1·8. Eighty-seven per cent of respondents were satisfied with this item as the following replies indicate:

There is a nice relaxed atmosphere in the school. Discipline is enforced by a very understanding principal;

The children are not unduly bold and discipline is not that of an iron hand.

The following replies illustrate the problems of those who said they were not satisfied with discipline:

—Discipline is rigid: there is little trouble teaching, but this is not satisfactory as a means of developing a child's individuality;

—Discipline seems to be getting more difficult every year.

(vii) *Hours of Work.* Score 1·8. Ninety per cent of all respondents said they were satisfied with their hours of work. A number however pointed out that although the hours were relatively short the work was tiring.

(viii) *Relations with Inspectors.* Score 1·9. Eighty-seven per cent of respondents said they were satisfied with relations with inspectors. Replies such as the following were common:

—They tend to be more helpful and constructive than formerly;

—They are very reasonable, provided an honest attempt is
made;
—I have found inspectors understanding and co-operative;
—If I work honestly, the inspector seldom finds fault;
—Many inspectors are too 'Irish prone'. The present
inspector is a gentleman.

While having no objection to the inspector personally, a
number of respondents took exception to the inspection system
as such:
—Those I know are helpful but, in general, there is the
feeling that the inspector is there to check up on one—
which I don't like;
—I do not like the element of fear often inculcated;
—The whole inspectorial system is degrading.

A small number of respondents said they would like the
inspector to give more help on teaching methods:
—Instead of offering constructive advice they tend to pick
out your faults. One can't talk to them man to man;
—They ought to aid me on methods. They don't.

(ix) *Relations with Parents*, Score 2·2, and (xii) *Attitude of
Parents to Education*, Score 2·5. The question of parent-teacher
relations has been dealt with extensively in chapter VII. Most
complaints mentioned here centred on parents' failure to
appreciate the value of education, and were especially common
in replies of teachers in city centre schools.

(x) *Attitude of Pupils to Education*. Score 2·3. Sixty-five per cent
of respondents said they were satisfied with this item. The
following replies are typical of the reasons given:

—They are terribly open to all new knowledge;
—On the whole, they respond to any incentive (tests, prizes).

Some factors were mentioned as adversely influencing pupils'
attitudes to education:
—In this area I find it difficult to get any respect for the need
for education;

—There is a falling off from the very satisfactory level, I
point the finger at T.V.;
—They are eager on the whole but size of class does not
permit proper attention;
—Since most of them come from a poor area their aim is to
get out and find a job.

(xi) *Respect and Recognition from the Public*. Score 2·4. Sixty per
cent of respondents said they were satisfied with this item.
However, a relatively large number (20 per cent) said they
were not interested in respect from the public:
—Who cares about the public?
—Teachers are not looking for respect from the public;
—I am not very worried about it as it doesn't count very
much.

Others referred to the public image they felt the teacher had:
We seem to be public enemy No. 1 (overpaid and tyrants);
—The image of the National Teacher is as though he were the
poor relation of other members of the teaching profession;
—'Teachers have the easiest job going,' I hear people say.
I wish some of them would try it for a while;
—There is a lack of understanding—teachers' motives are
often suspect;
—The public don't realize the importance of our work and
our influence on the children, and think our holidays too
long and our day too short.

(xiii) *Salary*. Score 2·5. Salary, especially for men, was one of
the sources of dissatisfaction mentioned more frequently. Forty-
seven per cent of respondents said they were dissatisfied with
salary (79 per cent of men and 33 per cent of women). Among
the reasons given were:
—Teachers are not at all paid properly for the amount of
time spent in training and the great responsibility;
—Teacher should not have to 'scrape';
—The basic salary is too low, and the incremental period too
prolonged;
—Unskilled workers are able to earn far more.

A number of respondents suggested that salary was adequate for women but not for men:

—Quite good for a single girl, not for a married man;

—The salary compares favourably with remuneration in other occupations for women.

A number of female respondents, however, made the following point:

—Men and women should have equal pay for equal work;

—There should be equal pay for equal work;

—'Married' extras should come from Social Service.

(xiv) *Curriculum.* Score 2·8. Considerable dissatisfaction was expressed with the curriculum. Sixty-eight per cent of respondents said they were dissatisfied with it. Slightly over half of those who complained said the trouble arose from the undue emphasis placed on Irish, while most of the others said that the curriculum was too restricted and did not allow for such subjects as art, and nature study. It is obvious that both points are related.

Among those who said that too much time had to be given to Irish the following replies are typical:

—I think that Irish gets more than its fair share of time, thus making the curriculum over-crowded;

—It is impossible to cater adequately for subjects other than Irish—time factor;

—Too much time is devoted to Irish; other subjects must suffer. Over thirty years, 80 per cent of my pupils have emigrated, and I think if we had spent less time on Irish they would have been better prepared for life abroad;

—I teach 5 year-olds and feel they should play more instead of trying to learn Irish—at least I spend so much time at it.

Replies of those who wanted a more 'liberal' curriculum are illustrated by the following:

—The curriculum is too narrow—no P.T., art, science or rural science;

—I would like to see art and nature study included;

—More emphasis on art, music etc. (exam problem) desired.

A small number of respondents from city centre schools pointed out that it should be possible to modify the curriculum to suit the area in which they taught:—

—There should be a special standard set for underprivileged children like ours.
—The curriculum is not suitable for pupils in our area.

(xv) *Training for Teaching.* Score 3.0. This was one of the items with which teachers expressed most dissatisfaction. Sixty-nine per cent of respondents said they were not satisfied with it (50 per cent of men and 74 per cent of women).

The complaints were fairly evenly spread between two points, possibly related; the demand that teachers take a university degree and demands for a 'liberalizing' of the atmosphere in the training colleges.

The following replies illustrate the first point:
—All teachers should have the benefit of university and a broader outlook on knowledge;
—A three year course, in conjunction with the university, is needed;
—A university training should be obligatory. Abolish the training colleges;
—Teachers should have university training to ensure 'status'.

Among those who complained about the 'atmosphere' of the training colleges the following replies are typical. All of these comments were made by women:
—I am very dissatisfied with their system, teaching, management and particularly the atmosphere;
—It's disastrous in women's training colleges. Students slide down to the infantile level;
—I spent most of my time writing notes. We were treated like children; one was often addressed as 'child'. The programme was too narrow and some of the lecturers were quite dull and uninteresting. We were not allowed to mix very much with other students and there were no debates, etc. On the whole the training we got was rather dull. I could write a book about this;

—My daughter refuses to go to training college because of segregation and boarding school conditions. She would be a very good teacher—it's a pity;
—The training course is very good, but does not allow for individual personality development;
—Too much discipline and regimentation.

A small number of respondents said that they thought the training of teachers had improved:
—My training left a great deal to be desired. I think to-day it has improved;
—From what I know of this I believe teachers get a good training now.

Three other teachers said that while they were not satisfied with the training available it was better than what other teachers received:—
—It's more than the secondary or vocationals get.

(xvi) *Opportunities for Promotion.* Score 3.0. Sixty-eight per cent of respondents said they were not satisfied with this aspect of teaching (83 per cent of men and 61 per cent of women). It will be remembered that 52 per cent of the sample taught in 'religious schools', and this meant that they could not become principals. Replies such as the following were typical:
—Very few avenues are open to lay teachers;
—I've been teaching 35 years (H.E.[13] in the old days) and am still an assistant;
—There are no opportunities and I feel I have the ability to supervise school work etc.;
—Responsible positions will always be held by religious in my school;
—On the whole there are too few opportunities—especially for men.

[13]Highly efficient. This system of rating teachers' work has not been in operation since 1948.

A small number of women said they were not interested in promotion:

—As a woman I'm not very ambitious, and teaching is rewarding in itself;

—Now, at this age, I'd prefer the work of teaching to that of a principal;

—There are sufficient opportunities for a married woman.

(xvii) *Size of Class*. Score 3.2 Eighty-one per cent of respondents said they were dissatisfied with size of class. Over three-quarters of these gave as their reason the fact that large classes prevented them from giving individual attention to pupils. The following replies were typical:

—Classes are much too large to give the necessary attention to each child, and especially to backward children;

—Large numbers make discipline and individual attention difficult;

Several respondents suggested that the ideal size of class would be 30 to 35 pupils:

—Classes still far too large—no class should have more than 30 pupils;

—I would like 30, would not be shocked if given 50. I have 40—reasonably happy;

—Class is much too large. I have 48. 30–35 should be quite enough.

A small number of teachers pointed out that there had been reductions recently in teacher-pupil ratio and that they hoped for further reductions:

—It has improved—I hope for further improvement.

(xviii) *Provision of Teaching Aids*. Score 3.6. This was the item with which teachers expressed most dissatisfaction. Ninety-two per cent of respondents said they were not satisfied with the provision of teaching aids and pointed out the lack of them:

—In the city schools, wall maps are rarely provided, there
are no history charts and rarely a musical instrument;
—Provision of teaching aids! —we have to buy even our
own *chalk*;
—Teaching aids are non-existent. On July 1st I went into an
empty classroom, no pictures etc.;
—*I never got one aid.* I make my own;
—In over 30 years I have never got any aid which I did not
buy.

A considerable number of respondents said that the Department of Education should supply teaching aids:

—The supply of teaching aids by the Department of Education is inadequate;
—Government grants for purchase of aids are insufficient;
—Some aids are provided by the principal. Lots should be
provided by the Department of Education.

As regards the type of aids desired the following replies are
illustrative:

—I would love some modern aids—film strips etc. for history
and geography;
—None whatsoever supplied. Tape recorder, slide viewer etc.
should be;
—Why are there no more free books, charts, film strips, tape
recorders?—What I could do with them!

Conclusion

It may be concluded from this chapter that about 85 per cent
of the national teachers in Dublin were satisfied with teaching
and felt that it had lived up to their expectations. Some city
centre teachers, contrary to expectations, achieved a high
degree of satisfaction.

Women teachers, especially those over 51 years of age, were
the most satisfied group. Teaching appeared to be seen as a
better job for women than for men, since 56 per cent of the male
teachers and 46 per cent of the female teachers said they would
either probably or definitely advise their interested son not to
become a teacher. The corresponding figures for a daughter

were 19 and 17 per cent respectively. Men were more dissatisfied than women with, among other things, salary, opportunities for promotion and respect and recognition from the public. They appeared to be more concerned with the tangible aspects of a successful career in modern society. These findings are similar to those of Kuhlen, of Bienenstok and Sayres, of Mason and of Getzels and Guba concerning teachers in the United States and to those of Rudd and Wiseman concerning teachers in Britain.[14]

Teachers' satisfaction with their work tended to be derived from working with children and from relations with their colleagues. The reasons respondents gave for finding their work with children satisfying often were that they felt that helping children was rewarding, that they related better to children than to adults and that children were 'responsive' and 'receptive'. The reasons they gave for finding their work group satisfying were the support and interest of their colleagues and of the principal.

This finding is very similar to that of Kuhlen who concluded his study by stating:

> One is impressed, first of all, with the degree to which teachers are 'people oriented'. When asked to indicate what features of teaching gave most satisfaction, the two items that emerged at the top of the list were that of seeing results of one's teaching in the growth and development of children, and the opportunities for satisfaction of affiliation needs with one's peers. The same finding appeared when the teachers were asked what they liked best about their current job. The two outstanding responses were related to the nature of the student body, and affiliation with peers, with satisfactions being derived from the activities of the occupation running a close third. These findings are directly in line with our expectation that teachers tended to derive intrinsic satisfaction from the nature of the work itself, rather than being oriented towards the conventional types of career development.[15]

[14]See Chapter II, pp. 13-16.
[15]R. G. Kuhlen, cit. sup., p. 199.

For Dublin teachers sources of dissatisfaction in their work tended to be those factors which they perceived as hindering their work with children and the achievement of their ideals. The two major factors were lack of teaching aids and large classes. Bienenstok and Sayres, and Rudd and Wiseman also found that large classes and lack of teaching aids were major sources of complaint for the American and British teachers they studied, though these teachers had smaller classes and more teaching aids than their Dublin counterparts. It is not very clear how this similarity should be interpreted. It may be that size of class and teaching aids, being more visible aspects of teaching, become the focus of unarticulated dissatisfactions. Or, it may be that having small classes and sufficient teaching aids are seen by teachers as the necessary requirements for professional work and that the desired limits have not yet been reached, even in America or England.

In Dublin the problem is probably more serious and requires immediate attention. Dublin teachers clearly feel strongly that they could do better work if the size of classes was reduced and if they were provided with teaching aids.

CHAPTER IX

CONCLUSION

THIS was a study of national teachers and national teaching organized around a number of social science concepts. The first was that of role. Teachers were asked by means of a role definition instrument what emphasis they put on different aspects of a teacher's work. The relationships between teachers and others in related positions, such as the inspector and manager, were examined by means of the concept role-set. Role-set was particularly useful in helping to focus on the occupation of teaching within the organizational setting of a school. One relationship in the role-set, that between parents and teachers, was studied in some depth. The social origins of teachers were examined by using two indices of social origins: social group origin and geographical origin. Finally the job satisfaction of teachers was investigated in order to find out the overall degree of satisfaction and dissatisfaction with teaching, and particular sources of satisfaction and dissatisfaction. Taken together, these findings present a coherent picture of national teaching and of lay national teachers in Dublin city.

This chapter attempts to interpret the findings of the study. Suggestions for further research are made and some practical implications of the study are considered, with the aim of stimulating discussion of the problems raised rather than supplying solutions to them.

Where comparable data are available, comparisons are made between the findings of this study and those of similar surveys carried out in the United States and Great Britain which have already been reviewed in Chapter II.

The chapter is divided into six sections:

1. Pupil-centred teachers
2. The role-set of the teacher
3. Parent-teacher relations
4. Job satisfaction
5. Social origins
6. Final comments.

Pupil-centred Teachers

The general development of his pupils was seen by respondents to be the teacher's greatest obligation. They felt that teachers were very strongly obliged to develop their pupils morally, socially and intellectually but that their obligation to teach the prescribed programme was not as great. It appears that a teacher's work was felt to centre almost exclusively around his pupils. Of all the positions related to the teacher only the pupil was felt by respondents to exercise much influence on the teacher's work. The aspects of teaching with which respondents said they were most dissatisfied centred largely on such factors as size of class which prevented them from giving more attention to pupils.

The conception of teaching as almost exclusively pupil-centred is probably necessary and desirable. However, in this chapter it will be shown that this exclusive attention to pupils may contribute to the problem of the lack of involvement of parents in the primary education of their children.

Certain features of national teaching are conducive to the development of this conception of a teacher's role. In national schools the same teacher teaches all subjects to the same class (with the occasional exception of subjects such as music) and a teacher may have this class for more than one year. One of the subjects on the curriculum is religious knowledge, and the teacher is encouraged by the Department of Education to foster at all times the moral development of his pupils.[1] Also,

[1]See Chapter III, p. 28 above.

no great importance is attached to examinations.[2] In these circumstances it is not surprising that the teacher sees his job in larger terms than simply teaching the prescribed programme.

An important question which might be the subject of future research is the possible relationship between the attitude of teachers and the academic achievements of their pupils. It would be of interest to discover whether the pupils of teachers who put greatest emphasis on the general development of their pupils would be less highly motivated to excel in particular subjects than the pupils of teachers who put greatest emphasis on teaching the prescribed programme. Research on this question could best be undertaken on a cross-cultural basis, possibly in the context of studies of the need for achievement.

The Role-set of the Teacher

By the role-set of the teacher is meant the relationships which teachers have with those in counter-positions. In this study the following counter-positions were focussed on: pupil, colleague, principal, manager, inspector, and parent. It was found that respondents were particularly satisfied with their relations with pupils, colleagues and principal, and satisfied with their relations with the manager and inspector. Relations with parents will be discussed separately in the next section.

One of the most important questions raised in connection with the role-set of the teacher was the extent to which respondents might be subject to role conflict from the possibly conflicting demands of the manager, principal and inspector. In Chapter III the duties of the manager, principal teacher and inspector were outlined, as were the rights of parents and others in regard to national schools. This formal outline was based on the *Rules for National Schools,* and it seemed from the description of the formal structure within which the national teacher works that he could be caught in the centre of a web of conflicting

---

[2]The abolition of the Primary Certificate Examination which pupils usually took on leaving national school and the provision of free post-primary education for all pupils without having to pass a scholarship examination, may almost eliminate examination pressure from the national school.

E

demands. However, it would appear from the findings of this study that national teachers in Dublin do not experience such conflicts because, despite the formal structure, they remain relatively independent in their work. Pupil was the only counter position felt to exercise considerable influence on respondents' work. Respondents said that the manager had almost no influence, while the inspector and principal had relatively little. Teachers appeared to feel free to follow their own dictates in working for the good of their pupils, hindered only by such structural factors as size of class and lack of teaching aids.

It will be remembered that respondents were satisfied with their relations with the manager, inspector and principal. It may be asked why this was so when they complained about difficult teaching conditions for which these people might be thought to have some responsibility. The manager is responsible for the building and furnishing of schools; it is one of the inspector's duties to supply the Minister for Education with the necessary information for the effective administration of the system; and the principal teacher, subject to the authority of the manager, is responsible for school organization.[3]

One possible interpretation of the attitude of teachers is that they feel that neither the manager, inspector nor principal have the power to do very much to improve teaching conditions. A more likely interpretation, however, is that the authority system in the school is such that if a teacher complained too much about school conditions the manager, inspector and principal might use their right to supervise his work more closely and so threaten his independence. To avoid this the teacher may be prepared to tolerate very difficult teaching conditions. This independence is particularly highly valued because of the type of relationship teachers feel they should have with their pupils. It is not suggested that the above situation is consciously brought about by the people involved in it, rather it appears to be the result of a particular type of authority structure and the importance teachers attach to independence in their work. Consequently, while teachers may complain of their working conditions at I.N.T.O. meetings or through a survey such as this,

[3]See Chapter III, pp. 26–7.

they may be very reluctant to make these complaints forcefully to their local manager, inspector or principal.

The situation regarding the supervision of teachers and their feelings of 'independence' is strikingly similar to that described by Alvin W. Gouldner as an 'indulgency pattern,'[4] one of the most important aspects of which, in relations between workers and management, is 'leniency' in supervision. In return for the non-enforcement of rigid rules and some other concessions the workers do not make too many difficult demands on the management.

The above is a tentative analysis of the 'independence' of the teacher. It could, however, provide the basis for further research which would specifically examine the role of the Irish National Teachers' Organization in relation to teachers' grievances. Further research might also study how teachers perceive the Department of Education and the extent to which the inspector is used to communicate teachers' problems to its officials and the Minister for Education.

In relation to the authority structure of the school the role of the principal teacher and how it may change in the future is worthy of note. It was pointed out in Chapter III that an important change was made in the duties of the principal teacher in the 1965 edition of the *Rules for National Schools*,[5] when included for the first time among his duties was '. . . the co-ordination and effective supervision . . .' of teachers' work.[6] It is likely that this change of rule will have a long-term effect on the role of the principal. Until 1965 the precise responsibility which the principal teacher had over the work of the rest of the staff was not specified, and in discussions in connection with this survey it was found that many teachers were still not aware of the change of rule. But, without adverting to the change, one teacher made a comment which may well be prophetic: 'Inspectors used to be the tyrants of national teachers in the old days, in future it will be the principals.'

[4] A. W. Gouldner, *Wildcat Strike, a study in worker-management relationships*, Yellow Springs, Antioch Press, 1954.

[5] See p. 27.

[6] *Rules for National Schools, op. cit.*, 1965, p. 72.

Parent-Teacher Relations

This study found that teachers in Dublin had little contact with the parents of pupils in their classes. When contact did exist it was informal, in that parents called to the school to meet the teacher. Very few parent-teacher associations existed, nor were they the form of parent-teacher relations favoured by teachers for the future. It would be superficial to interpret these findings as meaning that teachers are hostile to parents. They are more correctly understood as unanticipated consequences of the teacher's definition of his role exclusively in terms of his pupils and of his wish to maintain his independence.

It can be seen from the findings on the role definition instrument in Chapter VI that while Dublin teachers put great emphasis on the general development of their pupils, they did not feel that they had serious obligations to establish contact with the pupils' parents.[7] But recent social science findings have shown that a satisfactory home-school liaison is educationally important,[8] and some writers have suggested that the concept of teaching must be extended to include this dimension of home-school contact. To achieve this, Maurice Craft argues for the use of social work:

> This paper argues the case of closer links between parents and teachers at all levels, and suggests that an extended teaching role involving home-visiting and liaison with neighbourhood welfare agencies is a legitimate and necessary professional specialisation.[9]

But before many Dublin teachers will accept that they have an educational duty to involve parents in the work of the school, a change in their definition of a teacher's role is necessary. It is unlikely that this will be easily achieved as changes in socially defined role expectations are difficult to bring about and take time. Such a change may have to overcome the hostility of both parents and teachers, and misunderstandings between them.

[7]It is also of interest that not a single teacher suggested the possibility of teachers and parents working together to obtain better teaching conditions.

[8]See Chapter VII.

[9]M. Craft, 'The Teacher/Social Worker', p. 186, in M. Craft et al., (Eds.), *op. cit.*, pp. 186-208.

However, there are some signs of a desire for change among teachers. About half of the respondents said they would like more contact with parents, although some of this group of teachers foresaw difficulties in increasing parent-teacher contact, a half of them feeling that parents did not want more contact with them. This discrepancy between teachers' wishes and their perception of parents' wishes was greatest in poor city-centre areas where increased parent-teacher contact may be most necessary.

It is of interest to note that teachers in the United States who have much more contact with parents than teachers in Ireland find it a very satisfactory part of their work. Increased contact with parents should also be a source of satisfaction for Irish teachers. From the findings of this survey, however, it can be suggested that increased informal contact may initially have better results than the imposition of parent-teacher associations, to which teachers have such great objections. Maurice Craft's suggestion of an extension of teaching to home-school liaison is also worthy of consideration.

Job Satisfaction

Slightly under 80 per cent of men and slightly over 80 per cent of women were satisfied with teaching, but these figures are lower than those found for some occupations in other countries. Rudd and Wiseman found that about 92 per cent of the teachers they interviewed in England expressed satisfaction with teaching. Frederick Herzberg *et al.* concluded from their review of studies on the extent of job dissatisfaction in the United States that about 87 per cent of the working population were satisfied with their jobs.[10]

Sources of satisfaction for Dublin teachers were investigated. Relations with colleagues, including principals, and working with children were found to be the greatest sources of satisfaction. Studies of job satisfaction among teachers in the United States have come to similar conclusions.[11]

[10]F. Herzburg et al., *Job Attitudes: Review of Research and Opinion*, Pittsburg, Psychological Service, 1967, p. 6. The way they put it was '. . . a minimum of 13 per cent of our working population expresses a generalized negative attitude to their jobs'.
[11]See Chapter II, pp. 13-16.

While stating that they were satisfied with teaching in general, many respondents reported that there were particular aspects of teaching which caused them frustration and dissatisfaction. The two most common sources of such dissatisfaction were size of class and lack of teaching aids. For men, opportunities for promotion, salary and the curriculum also ranked high in the scale of dissatisfaction. Training for teaching was a source of dissatisfaction for all respondents, but especially for women.

This study found a consistency between how teachers defined their role and the satisfactions and dissatisfactions which they felt. They defined their role almost exclusively in terms of their pupils. The satisfactions they felt with relations with pupils and the dissatisfactions with factors which inhibited this relationship were consistent with this role definition, which might indicate that some sources of dissatisfaction emanate from the nature of the teacher's definition of his role.[12]

In relation to differences in job satisfaction between men and women it may be remembered that respondents were asked what advice they would give to their son or daughter if he or she was interested in becoming a national teacher.[13] A considerable number of both men and women said that they would advise their daughter but not their son to become a teacher. This may indicate that many teachers saw teaching as a good job for women but not for men. Some indications of the reasons for this can be obtained by comparing sources of dissatisfaction in teaching for men and women. Men were significantly more dissatisfied than women with opportunities for promotion, salary, the curriculum and respect and recognition from the public. Thus, perhaps, one of the basic reasons why teaching may not be seen as a good job for men is the lack of opportunities for promotion and the low salary.

To understand why this is so it is necessary to consider a person's occupational role in relation to his other roles in

---

[12]Undoubtedly personality characteristics are important in explaining individual variation in job satisfaction. Kuhlen and Mason conceived job satisfaction as the result of the motivations, needs or values which the individual brings to the job and the extent to which the job fulfils them.

[13]See Chapter VIII, pp. 90–1.

society. An individual's role in the wider society may define whether or not particular aspects of his work are felt to be of great importance. An example is sex role. Society may define the wider male role in terms of achievement, income and prestige in society, and men may be more dissatisfied than women with an occupation which lacks these characteristics. As Ireland becomes more industrialized and more 'modern' an increasing emphasis on achievement through promotion and a high salary is likely to make national teaching even less attractive to men.

While low salary is common to teachers throughout the world, the lack of opportunities for promotion in Dublin has some unique features which makes it a particularly acute problem. The great majority of teachers in Dublin are lay teachers, but over half of them are employed in religious schools, of which they cannot become principals.[14] The number of principalships open to lay teachers is thus very limited. Furthermore, as the larger schools are almost all controlled by religious, the principalships which are open to lay teachers tend to be those in small schools.[15] Patrick Duffy in his recent book on the lay teacher in Ireland argues forcefully for the employment of more lay teachers in religious schools,[16] especially in city areas.[17] This, however, would do nothing to increase the lay teacher's chances of promotion to the position of principal teacher in these schools. Instead, the question which may need to be posed is, under what circumstances could lay teachers become eligible for the position of principal teacher in a 'religious' school. While this study cannot answer this question, it does offer some relevant evidence in showing that lay teachers in Dublin are highly committed to the moral development of their pupils. It also indicates that increased opportunities for promotion may be necessary if national teaching is to be an attractive career for men. Finally, as the role of the principal teacher in the future is likely to involve increasing direct

[14]In 'religious' schools at least the principal teacher is always a religious brother or sister. See: Duffy, *The Lay Teacher*.

[15]See Table B.2, Appendix 4.

[16]He used the term 'Catholic' schools.

[17]Patrick Duffy, *op. cit.*

supervision of teachers' work it will be more necessary to recruit principals primarily on the basis of their qualifications and ability as teachers.

The position of vice-principal or special assistant should also be studied carefully, in order to investigate the extent to which it is seen as a significant promotion by teachers. In discussions with teachers the author found that promotion to that position is not always regarded as worthwhile. Two reasons were suggested for this: (a) that it was obtained automatically if a teacher had 'seniority' in the school and (b) that often no special responsibilities went with it. If further research revealed this to be the case, it might be necessary to alter the position radically.

Social Origins

Many teachers in Dublin have different class or geographical origins from those of their pupils. The question as to whether class or regional differences are sufficiently great in Ireland to have an adverse effect on teacher-pupil communication requires further investigation. It might be, however, that taken together both factors could give rise to a serious problem. Differences in regional accents, in both Irish and English, might add to the difficulties.

Related to the social origins of national teachers is the question of their recruitment and, in this connection, it is instructive to examine the position of the teacher training colleges. Because of the financial assistance given to students these colleges have had a special attraction for students whose parents could not afford to send them to university. This has resulted in keen competition for admission and very high entrance standards.[18] But the special position of the training colleges has also had an unintended consequence in that entrants are largely drawn from particular social groups and particular areas.

This situation may be regarded as unsatisfactory for a number of reasons. Firstly, the educational advisability of having teachers who differ widely in social and geographical origins from their pupils is open to doubt.[19] Secondly, teachers them-

[18]See *Investment in Education, op. cit.,* p. 120.
[19]See Chapters II, V and VII.

selves are unhappy about the teacher training colleges.[20] Many of them expressed a strong desire that national teachers receive a university degree and others, especially women, complained of the restrictive 'atmosphere' in the training colleges.[21] Thirdly, the privileged position of training colleges in the recruitment of very bright students could shortly be threatened by increasing aid to university students. The only satisfactory solution to these problems may be that the training of national teachers become part of the university system, in much the same way as training for other professions has.

Final Comments

This was a study in the sociology of occupations. It was an attempt to study a particular occupation, teaching, by using the concepts and methods of social science. But the respondents themselves probably gave the best overall impression of what national teaching is like in Dublin. At the end of the questionnaire they were asked if there were any further comments they would like to make on teaching, an opportunity which many of them used to sum up what teaching meant to them. Perhaps there is no better way of concluding this study, than by quoting two teachers who did so:—

It is a very rewarding vocation but also a strenuous one. It demands a lot of patience but, if approached in the right way, it lends plenty of interest and enjoyment.

Over the past few years I have met teachers from U.S.A., Finland, Germany, France and Britain. I encourage them to tell me about their work—Literature, Maths, Art etc. When they ask me 'what do you teach?', they never understand my answer—'boys'. They look overwhelmed when I explain how intimately I am involved with that psychosomatic entity called a Catholic boy, and that I teach him prayers, piety, and the 3R's—the lot. When I add the revival of Irish and the low salary, I have to work hard to convince them of my sanity.

[20]Some teachers may not be aware of very recent changes in the training of primary teachers. But while changes such as those in St Patrick's College, Dublin may improve the quality of the training programme they do not alter the basic position of these colleges.
[21]See Chapter VII.

APPENDICES
AND
BIBLIOGRAPHY

APPENDIX 1

ADDITIONAL TABLES

Appendix 1 contains tables of results not contained in the actual text of the report. Some of the results in these tables have been referred to in the text or presented in summary form. The following outline of this appendix may help the reader to locate a particular table in it.

Tables A.1 to A.17 are the detailed tables obtained from an analysis of replies on the role definition instrument (RDI). Table 6.2 p.49 in the text is a summary of the findings presented here.

Tables A.18 to A.23 contain details of the amount of influence respondents felt was exercised on their work by the incumbents of various counter positions. In the text these results are summarized in Table 6.3 p.58.

Table A.24 contains the mean, variance, standard deviation and standard error for each of the Tables A.1 to A.23.

Tables A.25 to A.32 give cross-tabulations of factors related to degree of parent-teacher contact.

Tables A.33 to A.38 contain details on the ranking of various forms of parent-teacher relations.

Tables A.39 to A.48 give cross-tabulations of factors related to level of satisfaction.

Tables A.49 to A.56 are concerned with details on factors which respondents said prevented them from achieving their ideals as teachers.

Tables A.57 to A.74 give details of the degree of satisfaction respondents expressed with various aspects of teaching. They are summarized, in the text, in Table 8.6 p. 95.

Table A.75 contains the mean, variance, standard deviation and standard error for each of the Tables A.57 to A.74.

Table A.76 contains details of location of home at birth of respondents related to occupational category of father.

TABLE A.1

Obligation to Ensure Pupils perform Religious Duties

Obligation	Men		Women		Total	
	N	%	N	%	N	%
Absolutely Must	12	25·0	22	21·4	34	22·5
Preferably Should	21	43·7	48	46·6	69	45·7
May or May Not	3	6·2	16	15·6	19	12·6
Preferably Should Not	8	16·7	9	8·7	17	11·3
Absolutely Should Not	3	6·2	6	5·8	9	6·0
Does Not Apply To Me	—	—	1	1·0	1	0·7
No Reply	1	2·1	1	1·0	2	1·3
Total	48	100·0	103	100·0	151	100·0

TABLE A.2

Obligation to Organize Games for Pupils after School

Obligation	Men		Women		Total	
	N	%	N	%	N	%
Absolutely Must	2	4·2	1	1·0	3	2·0
Preferably Should	19	39·6	11	10·3	30	19·9
May or May Not	20	41·7	46	44·7	66	43·7
Preferably Should Not	2	4·2	16	15·6	18	11·9
Absolutely Should Not	4	8·3	24	23·3	28	18·5
Does Not Apply To Me	—	—	1	1·0	1	0·7
Other	—	—	2	2·0	2	1·3
No Reply	1	2·1	2	2·0	3	1·3
Total	48	100·0	103	100·0	151	100·0

TABLE A.3

Obligation to Send Reports on Pupils' Progress to Parents

Obligation	Men		Women		Total	
	N	%	N	%	N	%
Absolutely Must	11	23·0	17	16·5	28	18·5
Preferably Should	28	58·3	52	49·5	80	53·0
May or May Not	8	16·7	25	24·3	33	21·9
Preferably Should Not	1	2·1	4	3·9	5	3·3
Absolutely Should Not	—	—	2	2·0	2	1·3
Other	—	—	1	1·0	1	0·7
No Reply	—	—	2	2·0	2	1·3
Total	48	100·0	103	100·0	151	100·0

TABLE A.4

Obligation to Give Individual Attention to Backward Children

Obligation	Men		Women		Total	
	N	%	N	%	N	%
Absolutely Must	16	33·3	57	55·3	73	48·3
Preferably Should	22	45·8	37	36·0	59	39·1
May or May Not	5	10·4	6	5·8	11	7·3
Preferably Should Not	2	4·2	1	1·0	3	2·0
Absolutely Should Not	3	6·3	1	1·0	4	2·6
Does Not Apply to Me	—	—	1	1·0	1	0·7
Total	48	100·0	103	100·0	151	100·0

TABLE A.5

Obligation to Invite Parents of Difficult Pupils to Come and See him (Teacher)

Obligation	Men		Women		Total	
	N	%	N	%	N	%
Absolutely Must	24	50·0	50	48·5	74	49·0
Preferably Should	18	37·5	45	43·7	63	41·7
May or May Not	4	8·3	4	3·9	8	5·3
Preferably Should Not	—	—	1	1·0	1	0·7
Absolutely Should Not	2	4·2	2	2·0	4	2·6
No Reply	—	—	1	1·0	1	0·7
Total	48	100·0	103	100·0	151	100·0

TABLE A.6

Obligation to Train Pupils to Think

Obligation	Men		Women		Total	
	N	%	N	%	N	%
Absolutely Must	41	85·4	95	92·2	136	90·1
Preferably Should	6	12·5	7	6·8	13	8·6
May or May Not	1	2·1	—	—	1	0·7
Preferably Should Not	—	—	—	—	—	—
Absolutely Should Not	—	—	—	—	—	—
No Reply	—	—	1	1·0	1	0·7
Total	48	100·0	103	100·0	151	100·0

TABLE A.7

Obligation to Arrange Parent-Teacher Meetings

Obligation	Men		Women		Total	
	N	%	N	%	N	%
Absolutely Must	1	2·1	4	3·9	5	3·3
Preferably Should	11	23·0	23	22·3	34	22·5
May or May Not	10	20·9	35	34·0	45	29·8
Preferably Should Not	12	25·0	18	17·5	30	19·9
Absolutely Should Not	14	29·2	20	19·4	34	22·5
Other	—	—	1	1·0	1	0·7
No Reply	—	—	2	2·0	2	1·3
Total	48	100·0	103	100·0	151	100·0

TABLE A.8

Obligation to Give Good Example to Pupils by his Behaviour outside School

Obligation	Men		Women		Total	
	N	%	N	%	N	%
Absolutely Must	27	56·3	65	63·1	92	60·9
Preferably Should	17	35·4	31	30·1	48	31·9
May or May Not	1	2·1	4	3·9	5	3·3
Preferably Should Not	1	2·1	—	—	1	0·7
Absolutely Should Not	2	4·2	1	1·0	3	2·0
No Reply	—	—	2	2·0	2	1·3
Total	48	100·0	103	100·0	151	100·0

TABLE A.9

Obligation to Live in the Parish he Teaches in

Obligation	Men		Women		Total	
	N	%	N	%	N	%
Absolutely Must	—	—	1	1·0	1	0·7
Preferably Should	7	14·6	9	8·7	16	10·6
May or May Not	22	45·8	51	49·5	73	48·3
Preferably Should Not	10	20·9	14	13·6	24	15·9
Absolutely Should Not	9	18·7	27	26·2	36	23·8
No Reply	—	—	1	1·0	1	0·7
Total	48	100·0	103	100·0	151	100·0

TABLE A.10

Obligation to Give Special Attention to Very Bright Pupils

Obligation	Men		Women		Total	
	N	%	N	%	N	%
Absolutely Must	4	8·3	11	10·7	15	9·9
Preferably Should	18	37·5	38	36·9	56	37·1
May or May Not	10	20·9	27	26·2	37	24·5
Preferably Should Not	9	18·7	11	10·7	20	13·2
Absolutely Should Not	6	12·5	13	12·6	19	12·6
Do Not Know	—	—	1	1·0	1	0·7
No Reply	1	2·1	2	2·0	3	2·0
Total	48	100·0	103	100·0	151	100·0

TABLE A.11

Obligation to Teach the Prescribed Programme

Obligation	Men		Women		Total	
	N	%	N	%	N	%
Absolutely Must	7	14·6	37	36·0	44	29·1
Preferably Should	27	56·3	51	49·5	78	51·7
May or May Not	8	16·7	11	10·7	19	12·6
Preferably Should Not	4	8·3	2	2·0	6	4·0
Absolutely Should Not	1	2·1	1	1·0	2	1·3
Does Not Apply To Me	—	—	1	1·0	1	0·7
No Reply	1	2·1	—	—	1	0·7
Total	48	100·0	103	100·0	151	100·0

TABLE A.12

Obligation to Develop the Moral Character of his Pupils

Obligation	Men N	Men %	Women N	Women %	Total N	Total %
Absolutely Must	35	72·9	88	85·4	123	81·5
Preferably Should	10	20·9	14	13·6	24	15·9
May or May Not	1	2·1	1	1·0	2	1·3
Preferably Should Not	—	—	—	—	—	—
Absolutely Should Not	—	—	—	—	—	—
No Reply	2	4·2	—	—	2	1·3
Total	48	100·0	103	100·0	151	100·0

TABLE A.13

Obligation to Try to Ensure that Pupils Grow up Good Christians

Obligation	Men N	Men %	Women N	Women %	Total N	Total %
Absolutely Must	35	72·9	89	86·4	124	82·1
Preferably Should	13	27·1	13	12·6	26	17·2
May or May Not	—	—	1	1·0	1	0·7
Preferably Should Not	—	—	—	—	—	—
Absolutely Should Not	—	—	—	—	—	—
Total	48	100·0	103	100·0	151	100·0

TABLE A.14

Obligation to Develop in Pupils a Love of Ireland

Obligation	Men N	Men %	Women N	Women %	Total N	Total %
Absolutely Must	24	50·0	49	47·6	73	48·3
Preferably Should	22	45·8	47	45·6	69	45·7
May or May Not	—	—	6	5·8	6	4·0
Preferably Should Not	—	—	—	—	—	—
Absolutely Should Not	—	—	—	—	—	—
No Reply	2	4·2	1	1·0	3	2·0
Total	48	100·0	103	100·0	151	100·0

TABLE A.15

Obligation to Give Good Example to Pupils by his Behaviour in School.

Obligation	Men		Women		Total	
	N	%	N	%	N	%
Absolutely Must	41	85·4	96	93·2	137	90·7
Preferably Should	7	14·6	7	6·8	14	9·3
May or May Not	—	—	—	—	—	—
Preferably Should Not	—	—	—	—	—	—
Absolutely Should Not	—	—	—	—	—	—
Total	48	100·0	103	100·0	151	100·0

TABLE A.16

Obligation to Help Pupils Become Good Members of Society

Obligation	Men		Women		Total	
	N	%	N	%	N	%
Absolutely Must	37	77·1	83	80·6	120	79·5
Preferably Should	11	23·0	20	19·2	31	20·5
May or May Not	—	—	—	—	—	—
Preferably Should Not	—	—	—	—	—	—
Absolutely Should Not	—	—	—	—	—	—
Total	48	100·0	103	100·0	151	100·0

TABLE A.17

Obligation to Extend his Teaching beyond the Prescribed Programme

Obligation	Men		Women		Total	
	N	%	N	%	N	%
Absolutely Must	8	16·7	17	16·5	25	16·6
Preferably Should	21	43·8	40	38·8	61	40·4
May or May Not	10	20·9	35	34·0	45	29·8
Preferably Should Not	3	6·3	3	3·0	6	4·0
Absolutely Should Not	6	12·5	7	6·8	13	8·6
Does Not Apply To Me	—	—	1	1·0	1	0·7
Total	48	100·0	103	100·0	151	100·0

TABLE A.18

Colleagues' Influence on Respondents' Work

Influence	Men		Women		Total	
	N	%	N	%	N	%
Very Much	7	14·6	14	13·6	21	13·9
To Some Extent	14	29·2	33	32·0	47	31·1
Slightly	18	37·5	26	25·2	44	29·1
Not At All	7	14·6	29	28·2	36	23·8
No Reply	2	4·2	1	1·0	3	2·0
Total	48	100·0	103	100·0	151	100·0

TABLE A.19

Parents' Influence on Respondents' Work

Influence	Men		Women		Total	
	N	%	N	%	N	%
Very Much	4	8·3	12	11·7	16	10·6
To Some Extent	4	8·3	26	25·2	30	19·9
Slightly	26	54·2	36	35·0	62	41·1
Not At All	12	25·0	27	26·2	39	25·8
Other	—	—	1	1·0	1	0·7
No Reply	2	4·2	1	1·0	3	2·0
Total	48	100·0	103	100·0	151	100·0

TABLE A.20

Principals' Influence on Respondents' Work

Influence	Men		Women		Total	
	N	%	N	%	N	%
Very Much	4	8·3	18	17·5	22	14·6
To Some Extent	20	41·7	39	37·9	59	39·1
Slightly	18	37·5	31	30·1	49	32·5
Not At All	5	10·4	12	11·7	17	11·3
No Reply	1	2·1	3	3·0	4	2·6
Total	48	100·0	103	100·0	151	100·0

TABLE A.21

Pupils' Influence on Respondents' Work

Influence	Men		Women		Total	
	N	%	N	%	N	%
Very Much	27	56·3	83	80·6	110	72·8
To Some Extent	10	20·9	13	12·6	23	15·2
Slightly	8	16·7	4	3·9	12	7·9
Not At All	2	4·2	3	3·0	5	3·3
No Reply	1	2·1	—	—	1	0·7
Total	48	100·0	103	100·0	151	100·0

TABLE A.22

Managers' Influence on Respondents' Work

Influence	Men		Women		Total	
	N	%	N	%	N	%
Very Much	1	2·1	5	4·9	6	4·0
To Some Extent	6	12·5	9	8·7	15	9·9
Slightly	12	25·0	24	23·3	36	23·8
Not At All	27	56·3	65	63·1	92	60·9
No Reply	2	4·2	—	—	2	1·3
Total	48	100·0	103	100·0	151	100·0

TABLE A.23

Inspectors' Influence on Respondents' Work

Influence	Men		Women		Total	
	N	%	N	%	N	%
Very Much	8	16·7	18	17·5	26	17·2
To Some Extent	18	37·5	50	48·5	68	45·0
Slightly	17	35·4	29	28·2	46	30·5
Not At All	5	10·4	6	5·8	11	7·3
Total	48	100·0	103	100·0	151	100·0

TABLE A.24

Mean, Variance, Standard Deviation and Standard Error
For Tables A.1 to A.23.

Table	Mean ($\overline{X}$)	Variance (V)	Standard Deviation	Standard Error
Table A. 1	2·3	1·2	1·08	0·09
Table A. 2	3·2	0·8	1·05	0·09
Table A. 3	2·1	0·6	0·81	0·07
Table A. 4	1·7	0·8	0·89	0·07
Table A. 5	1·6	0·7	0·84	0·07
Table A. 6	1·1	0·1	0·32	0·03
Table A. 7	3·4	1·3	1·16	0·09
Table A. 8	1·5	0·6	0·77	0·06
Table A. 9	3·5	1·0	0·99	0·08
Table A.10	2·8	1·4	1·18	0·10
Table A.11	1·9	0·7	0·84	0·07
Table A.12	1·2	0·2	0·40	0·03
Table A.13	1·2	0·2	0·40	0·03
Table A.14	1·5	0·3	0·57	0·05
Table A.15	1·1	0·1	0·92	0·07
Table A.16	1·2	0·2	0·40	0·03
Table A.17	2·5	1·2	1·08	0·09
Table A.18	2·6	1·0	1·00	0·08
Table A.19	2·8	0·9	0·95	0·08
Table A.20	2·5	0·8	0·89	0·07
Table A.21	1·4	0·6	0·77	0·06
Table A.22	3·4	0·7	0·84	0·07
Table A.23	2·3	0·7	0·84	0·07

TABLE A.25

Degree of Contact Respondents would like with Parents Related to Type of
Area from which Pupils were drawn

Type of Area	Degree of contact (percentage)			
	More	No change	Less	Total (N)
Poor city centre area	62·5	33·3	4·1	24
Corporation pre-1939 estate	53·3	40·0	6·6	15
Corporation post-1944 estate	56·6	43·3	—	60
Privately owned housing	37·2	58·8	3·9	51
Total	50·3	47·0	2·6	150

TABLE A.26

Degree of Satisfaction with Parents' Attitude to Education Related to Type of Area from which Pupils came

	Degree of Satisfaction (percentage)				
Type of Area	Very Satisfied	Satisfied	Dissatisfied	Very Dissatisfied	Total (N)
Poor city centre area	12·0	8·0	25·0	50·0	24
Corporation pre-1939 estate	—	20·0	53·0	27·0	15
Corporation post-1944 estate	3·0	43·0	38·0	13·0	60
Privately owned housing	21·0	55·0	23·0	—	51
Total (%)	11·0	40·0	32·0	16·0	150

TABLE A.27

Degree of Satisfaction with Relations with Parents Related to Type of Area from which Pupils came

	Degree of Satisfaction (percentage)				
Type of Area	Very Satisfied	Satisfied	Dissatisfied	Very Dissatisfied	Total (N)
Poor city centre area	17·0	50·0	21·0	12·0	24
Corporation pre-1939 estate	27·0	40·0	20·0	13·0	15
Corporation post-1944 estate	17·0	38·0	37·0	7·0	60
Privately owned housing	29·0	49·0	20·0	—	51
Total (%)	23·0	44·0	27·0	6·0	150

TABLE A.28

Factors preventing Teachers from achieving their Ideals, Related to Type of Area from which Pupils came

| | Factors preventing Teachers from achieving their ideals (percentage) | | | | | | | | | | | |
| | Parents a Factor | | | | | | | | No factors | Factors other than parents | No. reply | Total (N) |
Type of Area	Parents not playing their part	Interfering parents	Lack of Interest of parents	Lack of Parent-Teacher co-operation	Attitude of parents	Non-co-operation of parents	Home influence	Total mentioning parents as factor				
Poor city centre Area	4·1	4·4	20·8	—	—	8·3	4·1	41·7	20·8	37·5	—	24
Corporation pre-1939 estate	13·3	—	—	—	—	—	—	13·3	—	80·0	7·6	15
Corporation post-1944 estate	1·6	—	6·6	5·0	3·3	3·3	1·6	21·4	15·0	60·0	3·3	60
Privately owned housing	1·9	1·9	5·8	—	—	—	—	9·6	23·5	66·6	—	51
Total (%)	3·3	1·3	7·9	·9	1·3	2·6	1·3	19·7	17·2	60·9	1·9	150

TABLE A.29

Degree of Contact Male Respondents would like with Parents related to Degree of Contact they thought Parents wanted with them

Respondents—contact with parents	Parents—contact with respondents (percentage)				
	More	No change	Less	No reply/ other	Total (N)
More	44·8	41·3	3·4	6·8	29
No change	—	87·5	—	12·4	16
Less	—	66·6	33·3	—	3
Total	27·0	58·3	4·1	8·2	48

TABLE A.30

Degree of Contact Female Respondents would like with Parents Related to Degree of Contact they thought Parents wanted with them

Respondents—contact with parents	Parents—contact with respondents (percentage)				
	More	No change	Less	No reply/ other	Total (N)
More	55·3	34·0	2·1	8·4	47
No change	5·4	85·4	—	9·0	55
Less	—	—	100·0	—	1
Total	28·1	61·1	1·9	8·6	103

TABLE A.31

Degree of Contact Respondents thought Parents would like with them, Related to Type of Area from which Pupils were drawn

Type of area	Degree of Contact (percentage)				
	More	No change	Less	Don't know/ other	Total (N)
Poor city centre area	12·5	75·0	4·1	8·3	24
Corporation pre-1939 Estate	40·0	60·0	—	—	15
Corporation post-1944 Estate	26·6	60·0	1·6	10·0	60
Privately owned housing	33·3	52·9	3·9	9·7	51
Total	27·8	60·2	2·6	8·5	150

TABLE A.32

Percentage of respondents ranking (1-6) formal Parent-Teacher Associations related to type of area from which pupils came

Type of Area	Rank of Formal Parent-Teacher Association						No Reply	Total (N)
	Ranked 1	Ranked 2	Ranked 3	Ranked 4	Ranked 5	Ranked 6		
Poor city centre area	—	—	12·5	25·0	29·1	16·6	16·6	24
Corporation pre '39 Estate	6·6	6·5	13·3	6·6	26·6	6·6	33·3	15
Corporation post '44 estate	6·6	6·6	11·6	25·0	33·3	1·6	15·0	60
Privately owned housing	3·9	5·8	13·7	15·6	50·9	1·9	7·8	51
Total	4·6	5·2	12·5	19·8	38·4	4·6	14·5	150

TABLE A.33

Number and Percentage of Respondents who Ranked 'Formal Parent-Teacher Associations' 1 to 6

Rank	Men		Women		Total	
	N	%	*N*	%	*N*	%
Rank 1	2	4·2	5	4·9	7	4·6
Rank 2	6	12·5	2	2·0	8	5·3
Rank 3	3	6·3	16	15·6	19	12·6
Rank 4	10	20·9	20	19·4	30	19·9
Rank 5	16	33·3	42	40·8	58	38·4
Rank 6	4	8·3	3	3·0	7	4·6
No reply	7	14·6	15	14·6	22	14·6
Total	48	100·0	103	100·0	151	100·0

TABLE A.34

Number and Percentage of Respondents who Ranked 'Period of Ordinary School Time to be Allotted to Meeting Parents' 1 to 6

Rank	Men		Women		Total	
	N	%	*N*	%	*N*	%
Rank 1	7	14·6	22	21·4	29	19·2
Rank 2	16	33·3	29	28·2	45	29·8
Rank 3	6	12·5	20	19·4	26	17·2
Rank 4	7	14·6	11	10·7	18	11·9
Rank 5	7	14·6	10	9·7	17	11·3
Rank 6	—	—	1	1·0	1	0·7
No reply	5	10·4	10	9·7	15	9·9
Total	48	100·0	103	100·0	151	100·0

TABLE A.35

Number and Percentage of Respondents who Ranked 'No Special Arrangements but that the Teacher sees Parents if they call to the School' 1 to 6

Rank	Men		Women		Total	
	N	%	N	%	N	%
Rank 1	22	45·8	54	52·4	76	50·3
Rank 2	3	6·3	15	14·6	18	11·9
Rank 3	10	20·9	8	7·8	18	11·9
Rank 4	5	10·4	12	11·7	17	11·3
Rank 5	4	8·3	6	5·8	10	6·6
Rank 6	—	—	—	—	—	—.
No reply	4	8·3	8	7·8	12	7·9
Total	48	100·0	103	100·0	151	100·0

TABLE A.36

Number and Percentage of Respondents who Ranked 'Teachers to be available in the School one Evening a Month to meet Parents' 1 to 6

Rank	Men		Women		Total	
	N	%	N	%	N	%
Rank 1	11	23·0	11	10·7	22	14·6
Rank 2	5	10·4	15	14·6	20	13·2
Rank 3	14	29·2	22	21·4	36	23·8
Rank 4	6	12·5	22	21·4	28	18·5
Rank 5	5	10·4	17	16·5	22	14·6
Rank 6	—	—	2	2·0	2	1·3
No reply	7	14·6	14	13·6	21	13·9
Total	48	100·0	103	100·0	151	100·0

TABLE A.37

Number and Percentage of Respondents who Ranked 'Special Meeting to be Called Once or Twice a Year at which Teacher, Manager and Parents are Present' 1 to 6

Rank	Men		Women		Total	
	N	%	N	%	N	%
Rank 1	5	10·4	10	9·7	15	9·9
Rank 2	9	18·7	26	25·2	35	23·2
Rank 3	7	14·6	24	23·3	31	20·5
Rank 4	12	25·0	19	18·4	31	20·5
Rank 5	7	14·6	10	9·7	17	11·3
Rank 6	1	2·1	—	—	1	0·7
Other	1	2·1	—	—	1	0·7
No reply	6	12·5	14	13·6	20	13·2
Total	48	100·0	103	100·0	151	100·0

TABLE A.38

Number and Percentage of Respondents who Ranked 'No Opportunity be given to Parents of Meeting the Teacher' 1 to 6

Rank	Men		Women		Total	
	N	%	N	%	N	%
Rank 1	1	2·1	—	—	1	0·7
Rank 2	3	6·3	2	2·0	5	3·3
Rank 3	1	2·1	—	—	1	0·7
Rank 4	—	—	4	3·9	4	2·6
Rank 5	1	2·1	2	2·0	3	2·0
Rank 6	34	70·8	79	75·7	113	74·8
Other	1	2·1	1	1·0	2	1·3
No reply	7	14·6	15	14·6	22	14·6
Total	48	100·0	103	100·0	151	100·0

TABLE A.39

Age and sex of respondents related to level of satisfaction

Age and Sex	Level of Satisfaction (Percentage)					Total (N)
	Fully satisfying	Satisfying on the whole	Moderately satisfying	Most unsatisfying	No reply	
30 or under, Male	16·6	50·0	20·8	4·1	8·3	24
30 or under, Female	33·3	46·1	17·9	2·5	—	39
31-40, Male	—	100·0	—	—	—	2
31-40, Female	25·0	66·6	8·3	—	—	12
41-50, Male	18·1	63·6	18·1	—	—	11
41-50, Female	38·0	52·3	9·5	—	—	21
51-60, Male	25·0	50·0	12·5	12·5	—	8
51-60, Female	50·0	34·6	15·3	—	—	26
61 or over, Male	—	66·6	33·3	—	—	3
61 or over, Female	20·0	60·0	20·0	—	—	5
Total	30·5	50·3	15·8	1·9	1·3	151

TABLE A.40

Comparison of (i) all respondents and (ii) respondents from poor city centre areas at each level of satisfaction classified according to age and sex

Level of Satisfaction	Men under 40		Women under 40		Men over 40		Women over 40	
	All	City Centre	All	City Centre	All	City Centre	All	City Centre
Fully satisfied	15·0	—	31·0	60·0	18·0	50·0	42·0	78·0
Satisfied on the whole	54·0	50·0	51·0	—	59·0	12·0	44·0	22·0
Moderately satisfied	19·0	50·0	16·0	40·0	18·0	38·0	14·0	—
Most unsatisfied	4·0	—	2·0	—	5·0	—	—	—
Total (N)	26	2	51	5	22	8	52	9

TABLE A.41

Level of Satisfaction of Respondents whose Pupils came from Poor City
Centre Areas Related to Sex

	Level of Satisfaction (percentage)					
Sex	Fully satisfying	Satisfying on the whole	Moderately satisfying	Most unsatisfying	No reply	Total (N)
Male	40·0	20·0	40·0	—	—	10
Female	71·4	14·2	14·2	—	—	14
Total	58·4	16·7	25·0	—	—	24

TABLE A.42

Percentage Distribution of Respondents over and under 40 years by Level of
Satisfaction

	Level of Satisfaction (percentage)					
Age	Fully satisfying	Satisfying on the whole	Moderately satisfying	Most unsatisfying	No reply	Total (N)
40 or under	25·9	51·9	16·6	2·6	2·6	77
Over 40	35·1	48·6	14·8	1·3		74
Total	30·5	50·3	15·8	1·9	1·3	151

TABLE A.43

Percentage Distribution of Respondents whose Pupils came from Poor City
Centre Areas, over and under 40 years, by Level of Satisfaction

	Level of Satisfaction (percentage)					
Age	Fully satisfying	Satisfying on the whole	Moderately satisfying	Most unsatisfying	No reply	Total (N)
40 or under	42·8	14·2	43·2	—	—	7
Over 40	64·7	17·6	17·6	—	—	17

TABLE A.44

Extent to which Teaching had lived up to expectations Related to Age and Sex of Respondents

Age and Sex	Definitely yes	Generally yes	Generally no	Definitely no	Other	Total (N)
30 or under, Male	8·3	66·6	20·8	—	4·1	24
30 or under, Female	23·0	61·5	12·8	2·5	—	39
31–40, Male	—	100·0	—	—	—	2
31–40, Female	16·6	83·3	—	—	—	12
41–50, Male	9·0	90·9	—	—	—	11
41–50, Female	19·0	76·1	4·7	—	—	21
51–60, Male	—	62·5	25·0	12·5	—	8
51–60, Female	38·4	46·1	15·3	—	—	26
61 or over, Male	—	66·6	33·3	—	—	3
61 or over, Female	40·0	60·0	—	—	—	5
Total	19·9	66·2	11·9	1·3	0·6	151

TABLE A.45

Advice Respondents would give to Daughters about becoming National Teachers Related to Area from which Respondents' Pupils came

	Advice					
Area	Definitely yes	Probably yes	Probably no	Definitely no	Other	Total (N)
Poor City Centre area	54·1	29·1	12·5	4·1	—	24
Corporation pre 1939 Estate	26·6	40·0	20·0	13·3	—	15
Corporation post 1944 Estate	43·3	43·3	5·0	5·0	3·0	60
Privately owned housing	35·2	43·1	15·6	5·8	—	51
Total	40·3	41·0	11·2	5·9	1·3	150

TABLE A.46

Advice Respondents would give Daughters about becoming National Teachers,
Related to Age and Sex of Respondents

Age and Sex	Advice					
	Definitely yes	Probably yes	Probably no	Definitely no	Other/ No reply	Total (N)
30 or under, Male	37·5	50·0	4·1	—	8·2	24
30 or under, Female	30·7	56·4	7·6	5·1	—	39
31–40, Male	—	100·0		—	—	2
31–40, Female	41·6	50·0	—	8·3	—	12
41–50, Male	45·4	36·3	9·0	9·0	—	11
41–50, Female	57·1	23·8	14·2	4·7	—	21
51–60, Male	37·5	12·5	37·5	12·5	—	8
51–60, Female	42·3	34·6	11·5	11·5	—	26
61 or over, Male	33·3		66·6	—	—	3
61 or over, Female	60·0	20·0	20·0	—	—	5
Total	40·3	41·0	11·2	5·9	1·2	151

TABLE A.47

Advice Respondents would give Sons about becoming National Teachers
Related to Area from which Respondents' Pupils came

Area	Advice				
	Definitely yes	Probably yes	Probably no	Definitely no	Total (N)
Poor City Centre area	33·3	20·8	25·0	20·8	24
Corporation pre 1939 Estate	13·3	26·6	13·3	46·6	15
Corporation post 1944 Estate	18·3	35·0	23·3	20·0	60
Privately owned housing	15·6	25·4	31·3	25·4	51
Total	19·2	29·1	25·1	24·5	150

TABLE A.52

Factors which Prevent Achievement of Ideals—Curriculum

Reason why Curriculum was a factor	Men		Women		Total	
	N	%	N	%	N	%
Too narrow	5	10·4	3	3·0	8	5·3
Too much time on Irish	3	6·3	7	6·8	10	6·6
Examinations	1	2·1	2	2·0	3	2·0
Over-emphasis on written Irish	1	2·1	—	—	1	0·7
Other	3	6·2	2	2·0	5	3·3
Total	13	27·0	14	14·0	27	18·0

TABLE A.53

Factors which Prevent Achievement of Ideals—Management and Administration of School

Reason why Management and administration of school were a factor	Men		Women		Total	
	N	%	N	%	N	%
Poor school buildings	2	4·2	3	3·0	5	3·3
Poor heating and cleaning	1	2·1	3	3·0	4	2·6
Little freedom in organizing activities	1	2·1	1	1·0	2	1·3
Attitude of Principal	—	—	3	3·0	3	2·0
Attitude of Inspector	2	4·2	—	—	2	1·3
A rigid system	3	6·3	—	—	3	2·0
Total	9	19·0	10	10·0	19	13·0

TABLE A.54

Factors which prevent Achievments of Ideals—Class

Reason why Class was a Factor	Men		Women		Total	
	N	%	N	%	N	%
Too big	17	35·4	29	28·2	46	30·5
Too big for good teaching	1	2·1	2	2·0	3	2·0
Too big for individual attention	—	—	5	4·9	5	3·3
Two classes or over to teach	2	4·2	—	—	2	1·3
Total	20	42·0	36	35·0	56	37·0

TABLE A.55

Other Factors which prevent Achievement of Ideals

Other Factors	Men		Women		Total	
	N	%	N	%	N	%
Inadequate training	2	4·2	1	1·0	3	2·0
Lack of refresher courses	1	2·1	—	—	1	0·7
Personal inadequacies	1	2·1	2	2·0	3	2·0
District in which school is situated	1	2·1	1	1·0	2	1·3
Lack of compulsory refresher courses	—	—	1	1·0	1	0·7
Lack of funds	—	—	1	1·0	1	0·7
Not enough time in school to achieve all teachers would like	1	2·1	1	1·0	2	1·3
Lack of freedom from financial preoccupations	3	6·3	2	2·0	5	3·3
Out-of-date attitude of Department of Education	1	2·1	—	—	1	0·7
Other	5	10·4	4	3·9	9	6·0
Total	15	31·0	13	13·0	28	19·0

G

TABLE A.56

Breakdown of the number of Respondents classified by age and sex who said there were no Factors preventing them from achieving their ideals

Men 30–	Women 30–	Men 31–40	Women 31–40	Men 41–50	Women 41–50	Men 51–60	Women 51–60	Men 60+	Women 60+	N
12·5%	17·9%	—	16·6%	—	23·8%	—	34·6%	—	—	26

TABLE A.57

Satisfaction with Relations with Parents

	Men N	Men %	Women N	Women %	Total N	Total %
Very Satisfied	8	16·7	26	25·2	34	22·5
Satisfied	18	37·6	48	46·6	66	43·7
Dissatisfied	17	35·4	23	21·4	40	26·5
Very Dissatisfied	5	10·4	4	4·0	9	5·9
No reply	—	—	2	2·0	2	1·3
Total	48	100·0	103	100·0	151	100·0

TABLE A.58

Satisfaction with Holidays

	Men N	Men %	Women N	Women %	Total N	Total %
Very Satisfied	29	60·5	49	47·6	78	51·6
Satisfied	15	31·3	47	45·6	62	41·0
Dissatisfied	3	6·2	3	3·0	6	4·0
Very Dissatisfied	1	2·1	1	1·0	2	1·3
No reply	—	—	3	3·0	3	2·0
Total	48	100·0	103	100·0	151	100·0

TABLE A.59

Satisfaction with Curriculum

	Men N	Men %	Women N	Women %	Total N	Total %
Very Satisfied	1	2·1	7	6·9	8	5·3
Satisfied	6	12·5	29	28·1	35	23·1
Dissatisfied	27	56·2	47	45·7	74	49·0
Very Dissatisfied	13	27·2	15	14·6	28	18·5
No reply	1	2·1	5	4·9	6	4·0
Total	48	100·0	103	100·0	151	100·0

TABLE A.60

Satisfaction with Salary

	Men N	Men %	Women N	Women %	Total N	Total %
Very Satisfied	2	4·2	7	6·9	9	5·9
Satisfied	8	16·6	59	57·3	67	44·4
Dissatisfied	23	47·9	31	30·1	54	35·8
Very Dissatisfied	15	31·3	3	3·0	18	11·9
No reply	—	—	3	3·0	3	2·0
Total	48	100·0	103	100·0	151	100·0

TABLE A.61

Satisfaction with Hours of Work

	Men N	Men %	Women N	Women %	Total N	Total %
Very Satisfied	20	41·7	29	28·1	49	32·5
Satisfied	25	52·1	63	61·1	88	58·2
Dissatisfied	2	4·2	9	8·8	11	7·3
Very Dissatisfied	1	2·1	1	1·0	2	1·3
No reply	—	—	1	1·0	1	0·7
Total	48	100·0	103	100·0	151	100·0

TABLE A.62

Satisfaction with Size of Class

	Men		Women		Total	
	N	%	N	%	N	%
Very Satisfied	2	4·2	8	7·8	10	6·6
Satisfied	10	20·8	8	7·8	18	12·0
Dissatisfied	16	33·3	36	35·0	52	34·4
Very Dissatisfied	20	41·7	50	48·6	70	46·3
No reply	—		1	1·0	1	0·7
Total	48	100·0	103	100·0	151	100·0

TABLE A.63

Satisfaction with Relations with Inspector

	Men		Women		Total	
	N	%	N	%	N	%
Very Satisfied	13	27·1	26	25·2	39	25·8
Satisfied	29	60·4	64	62·1	93	61·6
Dissatisfied	3	6·2	8	7·8	11	7·3
Very Dissatisfied	3	6·2	3	3·0	6	4·0
No reply	—		2	2·0	2	1·3
Total	48	100·0	103	100·0	151	100·0

TABLE A.64

Satisfaction with Respect and Recognition from the Public

	Men		Women		Total	
	N	%	N	%	N	%
Very Satisfied	2	4·2	12	11·6	14	9·3
Satisfied	21	43·8	56	54·4	77	51·0
Dissatisfied	11	23·0	16	15·6	27	17·9
Very Dissatisfied	11	23·0	11	10·7	22	14·6
Other	2	4·2	3	3·0	5	3·3
No reply	1	2·1	5	4·9	6	4·0
Total	48	100·0	103	100·0	151	100·0

TABLE A.65

Satisfaction with Relations with Colleagues

	Men		Women		Total	
	N	%	*N*	%	*N*	%
Very Satisfied	32	66·7	70	68·0	102	67·5
Satisfied	15	31·3	30	29·1	45	29·8
Dissatisfied	1	2·1	1	1·0	2	1·3
Very Dissatisfied	—	—	1	1·0	1	0·7
No reply	—	—	1	1·0	1	0·7
Total	48	100·0	103	100·0	151	100·0

TABLE A.66

Satisfaction with Opportunities for Promotion

	Men		Women		Total	
	N	%	*N*	%	*N*	%
Very Satisfied	2	4·2	3	3·0	5	3·3
Satisfied	5	10·4	34	33·0	39	25·8
Dissatisfied	16	33·3	35	34·0	51	33·8
Very Dissatisfied	24	50·0	28	27·2	52	34·4
Other	—	—	1	1·0	1	0·7
No reply	1	2·1	2	2·0	3	2·0
Total	48	100·0	103	100·0	151	100·0

TABLE A.67

Satisfaction with provision of Teaching Aids

	Men		Women		Total	
	N	%	*N*	%	*N*	%
Very Satisfied	2	4·2	2	2·0	4	2·6
Satisfied	—	—	6	5·8	6	4·0
Dissatisfied	12	25·0	28	27·2	40	26·5
Very Dissatisfied	34	70·8	65	63·1	99	65·6
No Reply	—	—	2	2·0	2	1·3
Total	48	100·0	103	100·0	151	100·0

TABLE A.68

Satisfaction with working with Children

	Men		Women		Total	
	N	%	*N*	%	*N*	%
Very Satisfied	21	43·8	57	55·3	78	51·7
Satisfied	24	50·0	39	37·9	63	41·7
Dissatisfied	1	2·1	5	4·9	6	4·0
Very Dissatisfied	1	2·1	1	1·0	2	1·3
Other	1	2·1	—	—	1	0·7
No reply	—	—	1	1·0	1	0·7
Total	48	100·0	103	100·0	151	100·0

TABLE A.69

Satisfaction with Relations with Principal

	Men		Women		Total	
	N	%	*N*	%	*N*	%
Very Satisfied	30	62·5	62	60·2	92	60·9
Satisfied	13	27·1	32	31·1	45	29·8
Dissatisfied	5	10·4	4	3·9	9	6·0
Very Dissatisfied	—	—	2	2·0	2	1·3
No reply	—	—	3	3·0	3	2·0
Total	48	100·0	103	100·0	151	100·0

TABLE A.70

Satisfaction with attitude of Parents to Education

	Men		Women		Total	
	N	%	*N*	%	*N*	%
Very Satisfied	4	8·3	12	11·7	16	10·6
Satisfied	14	29·2	46	44·7	60	39·7
Dissatisfied	19	39·6	30	29·1	49	32·4
Very Dissatisfied	10	20·9	14	13·6	24	15·9
No reply	1	2·1	1	1·0	2	1·3
Total	48	100·0	103	100·0	151	100·0

TABLE A.71

Satisfaction with attitude of Pupils to Education

	Men		Women		Total	
	N	%	N	%	N	%
Very Satisfied	4	8·3	15	14·6	19	12·6
Satisfied	20	41·7	59	57·3	79	52·3
Dissatisfied	18	37·5	22	21·4	40	26·5
Very Dissatisfied	4	8·3	6	5·8	10	6·6
No reply	2	4·2	1	1·0	3	2·0
Total	48	100·0	103	100·0	151	100·0

TABLE A.72

Satisfaction with Discipline in School

	Men		Women		Total	
	N	%	N	%	N	%
Very Satisfied	15	31·3	39	37·9	54	35·8
Satisfied	28	58·3	50	48·5	78	51·7
Dissatisfied	2	4·2	10	9·7	12	7·9
Very Dissatisfied	2	4·2	1	1·0	3	2·0
Other	—	—	1	1·0	1	0·7
No reply	1	2·1	2	2·0	3	2·0
Total	48	100·0	103	100·0	151	100·0

TABLE A.73

Satisfaction with Training for Teaching

	Men		Women		Total	
	N	%	N	%	N	%
Very Satisfied	1	2·1	4	3·9	5	3·3
Satisfied	16	33·3	17	16·5	33	21·9
Dissatisfied	17	35·4	41	39·8	58	38·4
Very Dissatisfied	12	25·0	35	34·0	47	31·1
Other	1	2·1	2	2·0	3	2·0
No reply	1	2·1	4	3·9	5	3·3
Total	48	100·0	103	100·0	151	100·0

TABLE A.74

Satisfaction with Relations with Manager

	Men		Women		Total	
	N	%	N	%	N	%
Very Satisfied	20	41·7	50	48·5	70	46·4
Satisfied	20	41·7	38	36·9	58	38·4
Dissatisfied	4	8·3	7	6·8	11	7·3
Very Dissatisfied	3	6·3	4	3·9	7	4·6
Other	—	—	2	2·0	2	1·3
No reply	1	2·1	2	2·0	3	2·0
Total	48	100·0	103	100·0	151	100·0

TABLE A.75

Mean, Variance, Standard Deviation and Standard Error for Tables A.57—A.74

Table	Mean ($\overline{X}$)	Variance (V)	Standard Deviation	Standard Error
Table A.57	2·2	0·7	0·84	0·07
Table A.58	1·5	0·4	0·64	0·05
Table A.59	2·8	0·6	0·79	0·65
Table A.60	2·5	0·7	0·86	0·71
Table A.61	1·8	0·4	0·63	0·51
Table A.62	3·2	0·8	0·89	0·73
Table A.63	1·9	0·7	0·69	0·56
Table A.64	2·4	0·7	0·82	0·07
Table A.65	1·3	0·3	0·54	0·04
Table A.66	3·0	0·7	0·70	0·07
Table A.67	3·6	0·5	0·78	0·06
Table A.68	1·5	0·4	0·65	0·05
Table A.69	1·5	0·5	0·67	0·05
Table A.70	2·5	0·8	0·89	0·07
Table A.71	2·3	0·5	0·72	0·06
Table A.72	1·8	0·5	0·69	0·07
Table A.73	3·0	0·7	0·84	0·07
Table A.74	1·7	0·6	0·81	0·07

TABLE A.76

Location of Home at Birth of Respondents related to occupational category of Father

Location of Home at Birth	Farmer		Professional Manager		Intermediate & other non-manual		Manual		Other		No Reply		N	
	Men %	Women %	Men %	Women %	Men %	Women %	Men %	Women %	Men %	Women %	Men %	Women %	Men	Women
Dublin (city and county)	—	—	17	25	33	25	33	—	17	25	—	25	6	4
Rest of Leinster	17	55	33	27	—	18	33	—	—	—	17	—	6	11
Galway, Mayo	60	38	20	31	—	23	—	4	—	—	20	4	5	26
Rest of Connaught	—	38	—	63	100	—	—	—	—	—	—	—	1	8
Donegal	—	—	—	50	—	25	—	25	—	—	—	—	—	8
Cavan, Monaghan	—	13	100	50	—	13	—	25	—	—	—	—	1	8
Clare, Kerry	30	44	30	35	20	13	20	4	—	—	—	4	10	23
Rest of Munster	29	60	29	13	18	27	18	—	6	—	—	—	17	15
Other	—	—	—	—	—	—	—	—	6	1	—	—	2	—
Total	27	38	27	34	17	19	19	6	6	1	4	3	48	103

Confidential

QUESTIONNAIRE ON TEACHING

Introduction: This questionnaire seeks information on several aspects of teaching. If you wish to make any additional comments or to expand your answer to any question please do so. There is a blank page attached to the end of the questionnaire for this purpose. While some questions are more thought-provoking than others, in general do not delay over any question.

Where boxes are provided after a question please put a mark (X) in the appropriate box.

Questions 1, 2 and 3 are purely factual. The information is used for classifying responses.

1.

	30 or under	31–40	41–50	51–60	61 or Over
Age					

2.

Male	Female

3.

Married	Single	Widow/widower

4.   How satisfying do you find your work as a teacher?

Fully satisfying	
Satisfying on the whole but not fully so.	
Moderately satisfying	
Most unsatisfactory	

5. In your present position as a teacher to what extent do the attitudes of the following groups or individuals influence your work?

	Very much	To some extent	Slightly	Not at all
Colleagues.				
Inspector.				
Manager.				
Pupils.				
Principal.				
Parents.				

6. Has teaching as a career lived up to the expectations you had for it before you entered it?

Definitely yes.	
In general, yes.	
In general, no.	
Definitely no.	

Question 7 is designed to ascertain what teachers feel are central obligations in teaching. It is also aimed at estimating the extent of agreement among teachers on these obligations. It is important, therefore, that you give your own opinion in answering this question.

7.   As a teacher, what obligation do you feel a national teacher
        has or has not to do the following, having regard to the
        current conditions in Dublin schools?
        (Please put a mark (X) in appropriate box, for each item.)

	Absolutely must	Preferably should	May or may not	Preferably should not	Absolutely should not.
Ensure that pupils perform their religious duties					
Organize games for pupils after school					
Send reports on pupils' progress to parents.					
Give individual attention to backward children					
Invite parents of difficult pupils to come and see him					
Train pupils to think.					
Organize parent-teacher meetings.					
Give good example to pupils by his behaviour outside school.					
Live in the parish he teaches in.					
Give special attention to very bright pupils.					

Teach the prescribed programme.					
Develop the moral character of his pupils.					
Try to ensure that pupils grow up good Christians.					
Develop in the pupils a love of Ireland.					
Give good example to pupils by his behaviour in school.					
Help pupils become good members of society.					
Extend his teaching beyond the prescribed programme.					

If you wish to comment on any of the above or to mention any other obligations of a teacher please do so here:—

The purpose of question 8 is to discover what teachers feel is expected from them by others concerned with education.

8.   Please indicate in a few words what you think is chiefly expected from you, as a teacher, by the following:
(In all cases please answer in terms of your present position.)

Parents :—

Colleagues :—

Pupils :—

Inspector :—

Manager :—

Principal :—

9(a).   Are there factors which prevent your achieving your ideals as a teacher?

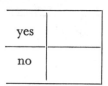

yes	
no	

IF YES   (b) What are these factors?

10.   If you had a daughter who was interested in becoming a national teacher, and had the ability to do so, and if she were to ask you what she should do what would you say?

Definitely yes	
Probably yes	
Probably no	
Definitely no	

11.   If you had a son who was interested in becoming a national teacher and had the ability to do so, and if he were to ask you what he should do what would you say?

Definitely yes	
Probably yes	
Probably no	
Definitely no	

12.   How much contact have you had with the parents of the pupils in your class, since the beginning of this school year?

(a) *In School*

Most of them called to the school to see me	
Some of them called to the school to see me.	
Very few of them called to the school to see me.	

(b) *Outside School.*

I met most of them outside school	
I met some of them outside school	
I met very few of them outside school.	

13. Is there a parent-teacher association or group, of any kind, in your school?

yes	
no	

IF YES, please give details:—

14. Would you like more or less contact with the parents of the pupils in your class?

More	
No change	
Less	

15.   Do you think the parents of pupils in your class would like more or less contact with you?

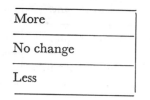

More	
No change	
Less	

16.   Rank the following forms of parent-teacher relations, by numbering them 1 to 6, according to your preferences.

	Formal parent-teacher associations.
	Period of ordinary school time to be allotted to meeting parents.
	No special arrangements but that the teacher sees parents if they call to the school.
	Teachers to be available in the school one evening a month to meet parents.
	A special meeting be called in the school once or twice a year at which teacher, manager and parents are present.
	No opportunity be given to parents of meeting teacher.

17.   Would you like to make any other comment on parent-teacher relations?

18 (a) How satisfied are you with the following aspects of teaching?

(b) Please indicate, briefly, your reason for your reply in (a)

	Very Satisfied	Satisfied.	Unsatisfied	Very Unsatisfied	Reasons
Relations with parents.					
Holidays.					
Curriculum					
Salary					
Hours of work.					
Size of class.					
Relations with inspectors.					
Respect and recognition from the public.					
Relations with colleagues.					
Opportunities for promotion.					
Provision of teaching aids					
Working with children.					
Relations with principal.					

Attitude of parents to education.							
Attitude of pupils to education.							
Discipline in school.							
Training for teaching.							
Relations with manager.							

19(a).   Below is a list of 8 occupations. Please rank them (1–8) according to the degree of prestige you think is accorded to these occupations in Dublin city.

	Clergyman.
	Dentist
	Doctor
	Electrician
	Garda
	Lawyer
	National Teacher.
	Veterinary Surgeon.

19(b) Below please rank the occupations according to the prestige you think should be attached to them.

	Clergyman
	Dentist
	Doctor
	Electrician
	Garda
	Lawyer
	National Teacher.
	Veterinary Surgeon.

20. How many teachers are there in your school?

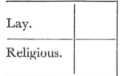

Lay.	
Religious.	

21. What is your position in the school?

Principal	
Vice-principal	
Assistant.	

22. What was your father's occupation?

23.   Where were you born and reared? (Please state county. Reared here means where you had your home for the first 10 years of your life.)

> *Born:*
> *Reared:*

24.   From which of the following types of area would you say most of the pupils in your class came?

Poor city centre area	
Corporation pre 1939 estate	
Corporation post 1944 estate	
Privately owned housing	

Thank you very much for your help. Are there any other comments you would like to make on national teaching?

APPENDIX 3

STATISTICAL NOTES

(a) *Details of Sampling.*

A list of all members of the Dublin City Branch, Irish National Teachers' Organization on 1 October 1966 was obtained. It consisted of 1,618 lay national teachers of whom 1,125 were women and 493 were men. From this list 1 member in every 9 (11%), or a total of 180 teachers, was randomly selected. Six teachers who taught outside Co. Dublin and 3 who taught in special and hospital schools were excluded, leaving 171 as the number to whom questionnaires were sent. Two questionnaires were returned incomplete; one without comment, the other because the addressee had retired from teaching and gone abroad. Completed questionnaires were received from 161 teachers. The replies of the following were excluded from the analysis: 9 principal teachers and 1 person who had left teaching. No reply was received from 8 teachers. Accordingly 151 is the number of replies used in this study.

Details of Sample

Initial Sample	180
Excluded before Dispatch of Questionnaires	9
Number to whom questionnaires were sent	171
Questionnaires returned, not complete	2
No reply	8
Replies received	161
Excluded from analysis	10
Numbers of replies analysed	151

(b) *Sampling Error.*

The sampling error of a percentage (p) of a sample (n) may be estimated, with sufficient accuracy, at the 95% confidence level by solving the following expression which includes correction for a finite population (N):

$$\text{Sampling Error} = \pm\ 1 \cdot 96 \left[\frac{p(100-p)}{N} \left(1 - \frac{n}{N} \right) \right]^{\frac{1}{2}}$$

As separate percentages were calculated for men, women and the total of respondents, sampling errors may be estimated for each of these groups, n being 48, 103, and 151 respectively. The error is greatest when the percentage is 50. Accordingly, at the 95% confidence level, the maximum sampling error for men (n=48) is 13·5%, women (n=103) is 9·1% and total sample (n=151) is 7·6%.

(c) *Significant Differences between Means and Variances of Men and Women in Tables 7.2 and 8.6.*

Significant differences between the mean scores of men and women were calculated (using a two-tailed test) by reference to the following formula :

$$\frac{S_1^2}{N_1} + \frac{S_2^2}{N_2}$$

where S_1^2=varience of men,

S_2^2=variance of women

N_1=number of men

N_2=number of women

Significant differences between the variances of men and women were calculated at the 5 per cent level by reference to the following formula: $\frac{\text{Larger } S^2}{\text{Smaller } S^2}$ and the F—Distribution table where S^2= variance.

APPENDIX 4

FURTHER TABLES

TABLE B.1

Number of lay and religious Catholic school units in the area covered by the Dublin City Branch, I.N.T.O.

Type of school	N	%
Lay Schools	129	53
Religious Schools: Nuns	84	35
Brothers	29	12
Total	242	100

TABLE B.2

Number of teachers classified by type of school, in Catholic school units in the area covered by the Dublin City Branch, I.N.T.O.

Number of teachers in school	Type of school (percentage)	
	Lay %	Religious %
1–6	69	5
7–12	25	51
13–18	5	27
19 and over	1	16
Total	100	100

TABLE B.3

Percentage distribution of lay and religious primary teachers in Catholic school units in the area covered by Dublin City Branch, I.N.T.O.

Type of teacher	%
Lay	81
Religious: Nuns	12
Brothers	7
Total	100

TABLE B.4

Percentage distribution of lay teachers in lay and religious Catholic school units in the area covered by Dublin City Branch, I.N.T.O.

Type of School	%
Lay	44
Religious: Nuns	47
Brothers	10
Total	100

BIBLIOGRAPHY

BANTON, M. *Roles—an introduction to the study of social relations,* London, Tavistock Publications, 1965.

BARON, G. and TROPP, A. 'Teachers in England and America', in Halsey, A. H., Floud, J. and Anderson, C. A. (Eds.), *Education, Economy and Society,* Glencoe, The Free Press, 1961, pp. 545-57.

BECKER, H. S. 'The Career of the Chicago Public School-teacher', *American Journal of Sociology,* Vol. 57, 1952, pp. 470-477.

BECKER, H. S. 'Social-Class Variations in the Teacher-Pupil Relationship', *Journal of Educational Sociology,* XXV, April, 1952, pp. 451-65.

BECKER, H. S. 'The Career of the Schoolteacher', in Nosow, S. and Form, W. (Eds.), *Man, Work and Society,* New York, Basic Books, 1962, pp. 321-8.

BECKER, H. S. 'The Teacher in the Authority System of the Public School', in Etzioni, A. (Ed.), *Complex Organizations,* New York, Holt, Rinehart and Winston, 1961, pp. 243-251.

BELL, R. R. (Ed.)., *The Sociology of Education, a source book,* Illinois, Dorsey Press, 1962.

BERNSTEIN, B., 'Social Structure, Language and Learning', *Educational Research* Vol. III, No. 3, June 1961, pp. 163-176.

BIDDLE, B. J., ROSENCRANZ, H. A., and RANKIN, E. F. (Eds.). *Studies in the Role of the Public School Teacher,* 5 Vols., Columbia, University of Missouri Press, 1961.

BIDDLE, B. J. and THOMAS, E. J. *Role Theory,* New York, Wiley, 1966.

BIDWELL, C. E. 'The School as a Formal Organization', in March, J. G. (Ed.) *Handbook of Organization,* Chicago, Rand McNally 1965, pp. 972-1022.

BIENENSTOK, T. and SAYRES, W. C. *Problems in Job Satisfaction among Junior High School Teachers,* Albany, New York, The University of the State of New York, 1963.

BLAU, P. M. and SCOTT. W. R. *Formal Organization,* London, Routledge and Kegan Paul, 1963.

170   TEACHING IN THE CITY

BLAUNER, R. 'Work Satisfaction and Industrial Trends in Modern Society', in Bendix, R. and Lipset, S. M. (Eds.), *Class, Status and Power*, Second Edition, New York, Free Press, 1966.

BLYTH, W. A. I. *English Primary Education—a sociological description*, 2 vols., London, Routledge and Kegan Paul, 1955.

BROOKOVER, W. B. *The Sociology of Education*, New York, American Book Co., 1955.

BROSNAHAN, J. 'The Sins of our Primary Education', *An Muinteoir Naisiunta*, (Irish National Teacher), 1, 2, Feabhra, 1956, pp. 18–26 and 1, 2, Marta, 1956, pp. 10–12.

Bunreacht na hEireann (Constitution of Ireland), Dublin 1937.

CASEY, T. 'Parent-Teacher Dialogue', *An Muinteoir Naisiunta*, (Irish National Teacher), 11, 5, Meitheamh, 1966, pp. 28–29.

CENTRAL STATISTICS OFFICE, *Census of Population of Ireland 1961*, Dublin. The Stationery Office, 1963.

CENTRAL ADVISORY COUNCIL FOR EDUCATION (ENGLAND), *Children and their Primary Schools*, (Plowden Report), 2 Vols., London, Her Majesty's Stationery Office, 1967.

CHANDLER, B. J. *Education and the Teacher*, New York, Dodd, Mead and Company, 1961.

COHEN, L. *An Exploratory Study of the Teacher's Role as Perceived by Headteachers, Tutors, and Students in a Training College*. M. Ed. thesis, University of Liverpool, 1965.

COLEMAN, J. et al., *Equality of Educational Opportunity*, Washington, U.S. Department of Health, Education and Welfare, 1966.

CONNELL, W. F. 'Portrait of a Teacher', *The Australian Journal of Education*, X, 2, June, 1966, pp. 123–132.

CRAFT, M., RAYNOR, J. and COHEN. L. (Eds.), *Linking Home and School*, London, Longmans, 1967.

CRAFT, M., 'The Teacher/Social Worker', in Craft, M., et. al, *op. cit.*, pp. 176–185.

CULLEN, K. *School and Family*, Dublin, Gill and Macmillan, 1969.

DOHERTY, M. J. 'Parent-Teacher Relationship', *An Muinteoir Naisiunta* (Irish National Teacher), 11, 9, Samhain 1966, pp. 11–12.

DOUGLAS, J. W. B. *The Home and the School*, London, MacGibbon and Kee, 1964.

DOYLE, L. A. *A Study of the Expectancies which Elementary Teachers, Administrators, School Board Members and Parents have for the Elementary Teachers' Roles*, Ed. D. dissertation, Michigan State University, 1956

DOWLING, P. J. 'Education in Eire', in *The Year Book of Education,* 1950, pp. 259–268.

DUFFY, P. *The Lay Teacher,* Dublin, Fallon, 1967.

EVANS, R. M. 'An Annotated Bibliography of British Research on Teaching and Teaching Ability', *Educational Research,* 4, 1961, pp. 67–80.

EVANS, R. M. 'Study of Attitudes towards Teaching as a Career', *British Journal of Education Psychology,* 22, 1952, pp. 67–70.

FAHY, C. 'Parent-Teacher Relationship in the U.S.A.', *An Muinteoir Naisiunta,* (Irish National Teacher), 11, 9, Samhain, 1966, pp. 25–26.

FITCHER, J. H. *Parochial School—a sociological study,* Indiana, University of Notre Dame Press, 1958.

FITCHER, J. H. *Religion as an Occupation—a study in the sociology of professions,* Indiana, University of Notre Dame Press, 1961.

FLEMING, C. M. *Teaching—a psychological analysis,* London, Methuen, 1958.

FLOUD, J. E. 'Teaching in the Affuent Society', *British Journal of Sociology,* 13, 1962, pp. 299–308.

FLOUD, J. E., HALSEY, A. H., and MARTIN, F. M., *Social Class and Educational Opportunity,* London, Heinemann, 1956.

FLOUD, J. and SCOTT, W. 'Recruitment to Teaching in England and Wales', in Halsey, A. H., Floud, J., and Anderson, C. A. (Eds.), *Education, Economy and Society,* Glencoe, The Free Press, 1961, pp. 527–544.

GAGE, N. L. (Ed.), *Handbook of Research on Teaching,* Chicago, Rand McNally, 1963.

GETZELS, J. W. and GUBA, E. G. 'The Structure of Roles and Role Conflict in the Teaching Situation', *The Journal of Educational Sociology,* 29, Sept. 1955, pp. 30–40.

GLASS, D. V. (Ed.), *Social Mobility in Britain,* London, Routledge and Kegan Paul, 1963.

GORDON, C. WAYNE, 'The Role of the Teacher in the Social Structure of the High School', in Bell, R. R. (Ed.), *op. cit.*

GOULDNER, A. W. *Wildcat Strike,* New York, Harper and Row, 1954.

GRAMBS, J. D. 'The Roles of the Teacher', in Stiles, J. (Ed.), *The Teacher's Role in American Society,* New York, Harper, 1957, pp. 142–179.

GREENHOE, F. *Community Contacts and Participation of Teachers,* Washington, American Council on Public Affairs, 1941.

GROSS, E. *Work and Society,* New York, The Thomas Y. Crowell Company, 1958.

GROSS, N., MASON, W. S. and MCEACHERN, A. W. *Explorations in Role Analysis—studies of the school superintendency role,* New York, Wiley, 1958.

GROSS, N. 'Some Contributions of Sociology to the Field of Education', *Harvard Educational Review,* 29, 4, Fall, 1959, pp. 275–287.

HALSEY, A. H., FLOUD, J. and ANDERSON, C. A. (Eds.), *Education, Economy, and Society,* Glencoe, Free Press, 1961.

HARRIS, C. W. (Ed.), *Encyclopedia of Educational Research,* Third Edition, New York, Macmillan, 1960.

HERZBERG, F., MAUSNER, B., PETERSON, R. O. and CAPWELL, D. F., *Job Attitudes: Review of Research and Opinion,* Pittsburgh, Psychological Service, 1957.

HOLINGSHEAD, A. B., *Elmstown's Youth,* New York, Wiley, 1949.

HUGHES, E. C. *Men and their Work,* Glencoe, The Free Press, 1958.

HUNTER, J. SCOTT. *The Beginning Teacher One Year Later,* Washington, Office of Education, US Dept. of Health, Education, and Welfare, 1962.

INTERNATIONAL LABOUR OFFICE, *Meeting of Experts on Teachers, Problems,* Geneva, 1958.

Investment in Education, Report, Dublin, The Stationery Office, 1965.

IRISH NATIONAL TEACHERS' ORGANISATION, *A Plan for Education,* Dublin, 1947.

KELLY, S. G. 'Attitudes of Teachers to Parent-Teacher Relations', *The Irish Journal of Education,* I, 2, Winter, 1967.

KELLY, S. G. *Role, Social Origins, and Satisfactions of Lay National Teachers in Dublin City—a Study in the Sociology of Occupations,* Unpubl. M. Soc.Sc. Thesis, University College Dublin, 1967.

KELLY S. G. and MCGEE, P. 'Survey of Reading Comprehension— a study in Dublin city national schools', *New Research in Education,* Vol. I, May, 1967, pp. 131-134.

KELSALL, R. K. 'Self-Recruitment in Four Professions', in Glass, D. V. (Ed.), *Social Mobility in Britain,* London, Routledge and Kegan Paul, 1954, pp. 308-320.

KELSALL, R. K. *Women and Teaching,* London, Her Majesty's Stationery Office, 1963.

KOB, J. 'Definition of the Teacher's Role', in Halsey, A. H., Floud, J. and Anderson, C. A. (Eds.), *op. cit.,* pp. 558-576.

KUHLEN, R. G. *Career Development in the Public School Teaching Profession with Special Reference to Changing Motivations, Pressures, Satisfactions and Dissatisfactions*, New York, Syracuse University, Institute of Research, 1959.

KUVLESKY, W. P., and BUCK, R. C. *The Teacher-Student Relationship*, Pennsylvania State University, 1960.

LINTON, R. *The Study of Man*, New York, Appleton-Century-Crofts, 1936.

LINTON, R. *The Cultural Background of Personality*, New York, Appleton-Century-Crofts, 1945.

MACNAMARA, J. *Bilingualism and Primary Education—a study of Irish experience*, Edinburgh, University Press, 1966.

MCELLIGOT, T. J., *Education in Ireland*, Dublin, Institute of Public Administration, 1967.

MCGUIRE, C. and WHITE, G., 'Social Origins of Teachers in Texas', in Stiles, L. J. (Ed.), *ibid.*, pp. 23-41.

MCVEIGH, H. 'Thoughts on schools', *An Muinteori Naisiunta* (Irish National Teacher), 11, 3, Aibrean, 1966, p. 11.

MARSDEN, D. 'Education and the Working Class', in Craft, M. et al., (Eds.), *op cit.*, pp. 48-61.

MASON, W. S., DRESSEL, R. J. and BAIN, R. K. 'Sex Role and the Career Orientations of Beginning Teachers', *Harvard Educational Review*, 29, 4, Fall, 1959, pp. 370-383.

MASON, W. S. *The Beginning Teacher—status and career orientations*, Washington, Office of Education, US Dept. of Health, Education and Welfare, 1961.

MAYS, J. B. *Education and the Urban Child*, Liverpool, University Press, 1962.

MAYS, J. B. 'The Impact of Neighbourhood Values,' in Craft, M. et al., (Eds.), *op. cit.*, pp.62-79.

MERTON, R. K. *Social Theory and Social Structure*, New York, The Free Press, 1957.

MOSER, C. A. *Survey Methods in Social Investigation*, London, Heinemann, 1958.

MULLIGAN, M. J. *Youth in a Country Town*, Unpublished M.Soc.Sc. Thesis, University College, Dublin, 1967.

NIEMAN, L. J. and HUGHES, J. W. 'The Problem of the Concept of Role—a re-survey of the literature', *Social Forces*, XXX, 1951, pp. 141-149.

NEVIN, M. 'Access to Secondary and Higher Education: the influence of non-economic factors', *Studies*, LVI, 223, Autumn, 1967, pp. 277-282.

NEVIN, M. *A Study of the Social Background of Students in University College, Dublin*, paper read before the Statistical and Social Inquiry Society of Ireland, Dublin, 27 January, 1967.

NOSOW, S. and FORM, W. H. (Eds.), *Man, Work and Society—a reader in the sociology of occupations*, New York, Basic Books Inc., 1961.

O BRIAIN, D. 'Programme for expansion', *An Muinteoir Naisiunta*, (Irish National Teacher), 7, 9, Deire Fomhair 1962, pp. 8-11.

OESER, O. A. *Teacher, Pupil and Task*, London, Associated Book Publishers Ltd., 1966.

O FATHAIG, P. 'Parents and Teachers', *An Muinteoir Naisiunta*, (Irish National Teacher), 11, 9, Samhain, 1966, p. 9.

O MUIREADAIGH, P. 'The Effective Way to an Educated Democracy', *Irish Independent*, 5 Sept. 1946.

OTTAWAY, K. *Education and Society*, London, Routledge and Kegan Paul, 1962.

PARSONS, T. *The Social System*, Glencoe, The Free Press, 1951.

PARSONS, T. 'The School Class as a Social System: Some of its Functions in American Society', *Harvard Educational Review*, 29, 4, Fall, 1959, pp. 297-318.

PHILLIPS, M. *Small Social Groups in England*, London, Methuen, 1965.

Report of the Council of Education, (1) *The Function of the Primary School*, (2) *The Curriculum to be pursued in the Primary School from the infant age up to 12 years of age*, Dublin, The Stationery Office, 1955.

RESEARCH DIVISION, NATIONAL EDUCATIONAL ASSOCIATION, *Economic Status of Teachers, 1966-67*, Washington, National Education Association of the United States, 1967.

RESEARCH DIVISION, NATIONAL EDUCATION ASSOCIATION, *What Teachers Think: a Summary of Teacher Opinion Poll Findings, 1960-1965*, Washington, National Education Association of the United States, 1965.

ROINN OIDEACHAIS, *Tuarascail, Tablai Staitistic 1964-65*, Dublin, The Stationery Office.

RUDD, W. G. A. and WISEMAN, S. 'Sources of Dissatisfaction among a Group of Teachers', *The British Journal of Educational Psychology*, XXXII, November, 1962, pp. 275-291.

Rules for National Schools under the Department of Education, Dublin, Government Publications Office, 1945.

Rules for National Schools under the Department of Education, Dublin, Government Publications Office, 1965.

RYAN, L. 'Social Dynamite—a study of early school leavers', *Christus Rex*, XXI, 1, Spring, 1967, pp. 7-44.

SARBIN, T. R. 'Role Theory', in Lindzey, G. (Ed.), *Handbook of Social Psychology*, Vol. 1, Cambridge, Addison-Wesley, 1954, pp. 223-258.

SCOTT, C. 'Research on Mail Surveys', *Journal of the Royal Statistical Society*, Series A, Vol. 124, Part 2, 1961, pp. 143-205.

SCOTT, W. H., HALSEY, A. H., BANKS, J. A. and LUPTON, T. *Technical Change and Industrial Relations*, Liverpool, University Press, 1956.

STILES, L. J., (Ed.), *The Teacher's Role in American Society*, New York, Harper, 1957.

SWIFT, D. F., 'Social Class and Achievement Motivation', *Educational Research*, February 1966.

TARPEY, M. C. J. *An Investigation into the Relative Importance of Intelligence in the Selection of Students in Irish Training Colleges*, Unpublished M.Psych.Sc. Degree thesis, University College, Dublin, 1963.

TERRIEN, F. W. '*The Behaviour System and Occupational type associated with Teaching*', Ph.D. dissertion, Yale University, 1950.

THOMAS, L. G. *The Occupational Structure and Education*, New Jersey, Prentice-Hall, 1956.

THOMAS, W. I. *The Unadjusted Girl*, Boston, Little, Brown and Co., 1923.

TROPP, A. *The School Teachers*, London, Heinemann, 1957.

VROOM, V. H. *Work and Motivation*, New York, Wiley, 1966.

WALLER, W. *The Sociology of Teaching*, New York, Wiley, 1965.

WARD, C. K. *Manpower in a Developing Community*, Abridged Report, Dublin, An Roinn Saothoir, 1967.

WASHBOURNE, C. *Involvement as a Basis for Stress Analysis: a Study of High School Teachers*, East Lansing, Michigan State College, Doctoral Dissertation, 1953.

WATTENBERG, W. and HAVIGHURST, R. J. 'The American Teacher—then and now' in Stiles, L. J., *op. cit.*, pp. 3-12.

WATTENBERG, W. W., et al., 'Social Origins of Teachers and American Education', Stiles, L. J., (Ed.)., *ibid.*,

WHITE, W. FOOTE. *Men at work*, Illinois, Dorsey Press and Richard D. Irwin, 1961.

WILLIAMS, R. M., Jr. *American Society*, New York, Alfred A. Knopf, 1965.

WILSON, B. 'The Teacher's Role—a sociological analysis', *British Journal of Sociology*, XIII, 1, March 1962, pp. 15-32.

WISEMAN, S. *Education and Environment*, Manchester, University Press, 1964.

WITTLIN, A. S. 'The Teacher', in Lynn, K. S. et al, *The Professions in America*, Boston, Beacon Press, 1967, pp. 91-109.

Year Book of Education, London, Evans Brothers, 1950-53.